DORLING KINDERSLEY  EYEWITNESS BOOKS

EXPLORER

Sealskin hood and mitten from Arctic expedition 1875-1876

Shoot and bark from *cinchona* plant from which quinine is obtained

Map showing Phoenicia on the eastern coast of the Mediterranean

Inca cup brought back by Francisco Pizarro

Captain Meriwether Lewis, American explorer

Spanish gold doubloons made from South American gold

DK EYEWITNESS BOOKS

Butterfly brought back from Australia by Joseph Banks

EXPLORER

Written by
RUPERT MATTHEWS

Charles Darwin's compass

Lodestone – naturally magnetic iron oxide – used by early explorers when navigating at sea

Christopher Columbus's ship – the *Santa Maria*

Cloves were brought back aboard the first ship to sail round the world

Dorling Kindersley

Indian wooden mask presented to Charles Wilkes and Meriwether Lewis

Shell necklace from the Cook Islands

Viking gold rings found in Ireland

DK

Dorling Kindersley

LONDON, NEW YORK, AUCKLAND, DELHI, JOHANNESBURG, MUNICH, PARIS and SYDNEY

For a full catalog, visit

 www.dk.com

Project editor Linda Martin
Art editor Alison Anholt-White
Senior editor Helen Parker
Senior art editor Julia Harris
Production Louise Barratt
Picture research Kathy Lockley
Special photography James Stevenson, Tina Chambers, Keith Percival, and Barrie Cash of the National Maritime Museum, London; Alan Hills, Ivor Curzlake, Philip Nicholls, and Chas Howson of the British Museum, London.

© 1991 Dorling Kindersley Limited
This edition © 2000 Dorling Kindersley Limited
First American edition, 1991

Published in the United States by
Dorling Kindersley Publishing, Inc.
95 Madison Avenue
New York, NY 10016
4 6 8 10 9 7 5 3

Dorling Kindersley books are available at special discounts for bulk purchases for sales promotions or premiums. Special editions, including personalized covers, excerpts of existing guides, and corporate imprints can be created in large quantities for specific needs. For more information, contact Special Markets Dept., Dorling Kindersley Publishing, Inc., 95 Madison Ave., New York, NY 10016; Fax: (800) 600-9098

Library of Congress Cataloging-in-Publication Data
Matthews, Rupert.
Explorer / written by Rupert Matthews;
photographs by Jim Stevenson.
p. cm. — (Eyewitness Books)
Includes index.
Summary: A photo essay about ancient to modern explorations of the land, sea, air, and space.
1. Discoveries (in geography) — Juvenile literature.
2. Explorers — Juvenile literature.
I. Stevenson, Jim, ill. II. Title.
G175.M35 2000 910'.722 — dc20 91-8428
ISBN 0-7894-5763-6 (pb)
ISBN 0-7894-5762-8 (hc)

Color reproduction by Colourscan, Singapore
Printed in China by Toppan Printing Co. (Shenzhen) Ltd.

Banjo taken on Ernest Shackleton's Antarctic expedition

Inuit (Eskimo) bone knives

Contents

Henry Stanley's hat

Early explorers

SIX THOUSAND YEARS AGO people knew little of what existed more than a few days' journey away from their own homes. Because they could grow all their own food and make everything they needed, they had no need to travel far. However, as civilization developed, so did the idea of trading goods with other countries. One of the earliest peoples to begin trading were the Phoenicians, who lived in cities on the Mediterranean coast of what is now Israel and Lebanon. The Phoenicians were expert shipbuilders and were able to sail great distances. They also realized that they could make money by trading. Between about 1100 B.C. and 700 B.C., Phoenician ships explored the entire Mediterranean, searching for new markets and establishing colonies. They even sailed through the Strait of Gibraltar to the Atlantic, and reached Britain and West Africa.

GLASS BEADS
Phoenician craftsmen were expert glass workers and were able to produce intricate pieces that were then sold abroad. This necklace was found in a tomb on the site of the ancient city of Tharros in Sardinia.

Demon head

Disk representing the world

EARLY MAP
This clay tablet was found in Iraq and shows the earliest-known map of the world. The world is surrounded by an ever-flowing stream, the "Bitter River."

COINS
Early Phoenician merchants swapped goods, but later traders used coins – pieces of metal stamped to show their weight.

Copper coin from Cádiz

Carthaginian coin from Spain

Silver coin from Carthage

Burial urn

Underground cellars

Phoenician inscription

BURIAL URN
This urn, found in Carthage, North Africa (near present-day Tunis), contains the bones of a child. Carthage was the main trading center for all Phoenician colonies. It was the custom there to sacrifice children to gods and goddesses; the bones were then buried in pottery burial urns in underground cellars.

BROKEN POTTERY
This piece of broken pottery is inscribed in Phoenician with the name of the powerful and beautiful goddess Astarte. It was found on the island of Malta, which lay on several shipping routes. Malta was colonized by the Phoenicians as a trading center.

118537

FOOD POWER
The Phoenicians shipped grain from Spain to many cities. Their control of the food supply made the Phoenicians extremely powerful.

Star

Crescent and disk

Lotus flower

Monkey

JASPER SEAL
Ornamental seals were favorite items throughout the Mediterranean. High-quality pieces like this were carved by Phoenician craftsmen from jasper mined in Sardinia, and shipped elsewhere for sale.

BRONZE BOWL
Phoenician trade helped to spread culture and ideas. This bronze bowl, made by a Phoenician metalsmith in about 750 B.C., is decorated with motifs used by the Egyptians. It was later exported to the Assyrian Empire, in modern Iraq.

COPPER CARRIER
This figure of a Phoenician merchant was found on Cyprus. He is carrying copper, which the Phoenicians collected from Cyprus to trade elsewhere.

WESTWARD BOUND
The Phoenicians dominated trade and exploration in the Mediterranean for several hundred years. As you can see from this map, they sailed westward from the ports of Sidon and Tyre in the Middle East, finding new peoples with whom to trade goods.

DEMON MASK
This terracotta mask, found in the tomb of a Phoenician on the island of Sardinia in the Mediterranean, represents a demon. It is thought that the mask was intended to frighten away evil spirits.

BALAWAT GATES *below*
This bronze plaque from a pair of gates was found at Balawat (present-day Qayyarali) in Iraq. It depicts Phoenician merchants leaving Tyre. They are loading goods onto ships, and then unloading them in a foreign country.

Silver coin from Sidon showing a Phoenician galley (ship)

Gates of Tyre

Loaded ships

Cargo being unloaded

Egyptian expeditions

The world's earliest civilizations, of which Egypt was one, developed in the rich lands of the Middle East. By 3000 B.C., Egypt had become a state, and numerous towns and cities sprang up in the fertile valley of the Nile River. According to Egyptian belief – as taught by the priests – the world was flat and rectangular; the heavens were supported by four massive pillars at each corner of the Earth, beyond which lay the Ocean – "a vast, endless stretch of ever-flowing water." At first, the Egyptians stayed in the Nile Valley, but they soon began traveling farther and farther in search of new peoples to trade with. One of the most famous Egyptian voyages was made to Punt at the command of Queen Hatshepsut (see below). Despite this expedition, Egyptian priests still asserted the existence of sky supports – they were just farther away than the priests thought!

REED BOATS
Before the Egyptians found cedar wood for building ocean-going boats, sailing was restricted to the Nile River. Nile boats were made from reeds lashed together to form a slightly concave (inward-curving) structure.

ROYAL CARTOUCHE
A cartouche is an oval shape in which characters representing a sovereign's name are written. This is the cartouche of Queen Hatshepsut.

Faience

Lapis lazuli

BEETLE RINGS
Egyptian rings were often made with a stone shaped like a scarab beetle. These scarab rings carry the cartouche of Queen Hatshepsut and belonged to her officials. They are made of gold, faience (glazed ware), and lapis lazuli that was imported from other lands.

QUEEN HATSHEPSUT
Around 1490 B.C., Queen Hatshepsut sent a fleet of ships southward through the Red Sea, and possibly as far as the Indian Ocean. The expedition found a country called Punt (probably modern-day Somalia, East Africa), where they were delighted to find ivory, ebony, and myrrh trees.

WOODEN SHIP *below*
After about 2700 B.C., the Egyptians began building wooden sailing ships capable of sea voyages. These ships sailed along the Mediterranean coasts to trade with nearby countries.

Bow (front of ship)

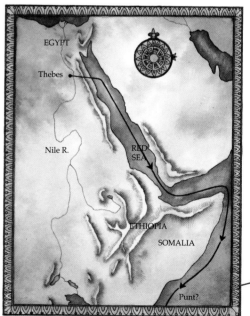

Map showing the route the Egyptians took to Punt

PRETTY FACES
Egyptian nobility wore large amounts of make-up, which they kept in containers such as this. Merchants explored many areas of North Africa and western Asia searching for cosmetic ingredients.

Thick rope pulled tight to stop the boat from sagging at each end

Blue faience

Ivory inlay

Ebony

GEM OF A BOX
This Egyptian box is
made of ebony wood
with an ivory inlay,
and may have been
used for keeping jewelry in.
Both ebony and ivory were among
the precious cargo Egyptian explorers
brought back from Punt.

Myrrh gum resin

MYRRH
Myrrh was
a vital part of
Egyptian religious
ceremonies.
Egyptian explorers
brought back myrrh
and frankincense
from Punt. In
addition to the gum
resin, they also carried
back myrrh trees to
plant in front of Queen
Hatshepsut's temple.

This copy of a tomb
painting shows
Egyptians making
piles of incense

Pellets
burned here

Container for
pellets of incense

BRONZE BURNER
Incense, such as myrrh and frankincense, was
burned at all Egyptian religious ceremonies and
was very valuable. This bronze incense burner
has a falcon head, and it may have been sacred to
the sky god Horus.

Falcon head

Cinnamon sticks

Mast

Stern (back
of ship)

SAUCY SPICES
Cinnamon spice was often
used in cooking by rich Egyptians. It came from
the coast of India; from there it was shipped by
Arabs to Arabia (pp. 18–19) for sale to Egyptian
merchants.

Steering oars

STRONG CEDAR
Sea-going ships like the one on
the left were built from cedar
wood, which the Egyptians
brought back from Lebanon.

Imperial expansion

THE MEDITERRANEAN WAS dominated by two great empires during the period between about 350 B.C. and A.D. 500. Alexander the Great, king of Macedonia (now part of northern Greece), conquered a vast empire which stretched from Greece to Egypt to India. The later Roman Empire was even larger, reaching from northern Britain to the Sahara desert in Africa, and from the Black Sea to the Atlantic Ocean. It was a time of great exploration and expansion, both on land and sea. Alexander sent ambassadors to the distant lands of northern India to establish contacts. Roman emperors sent many expeditions both into Europe and into Africa. Much exploration, however, was undertaken by private merchants and travelers; some evidence of their activities can be seen on these pages. One Greek merchant is said to have sailed to Iceland in search of new lands, and Romans traded with the wandering nomad peoples of Central Asia.

JASON AND THE ARGONAUTS
The ancient Greek legends of Jason – a heroic sailor who voyaged to many distant countries – were almost certainly romanticized accounts of real Greek journeys of exploration.

Alexander sent peacocks from India back to Greece

THE HAWK
This gold Greek brooch was found in Ephesus, an ancient Greek city just south of present-day Izmir in Turkey.

TRADING SOUTH
This small stone baboon was found on the site of Naucratis, a Greek colony in the Nile Delta. The colony was founded in about 540 B.C. by Greek merchants who traded for spices from Arabia and for ivory from Africa.

This map shows Alexander's route

ALEXANDER THE GREAT
In 334 B.C., Alexander, king of Macedonia, led a Greek army into the great Persian Empire. By 327 B.C., he had captured an area that stretched from Egypt in the west to the Indus River, Pakistan, in the east. The following year, he conquered parts of northern India before returning to Persia. His vast empire allowed Greek merchants and travelers to penetrate deep into Asia.

This coin shows Alexander attacking an Indian king

PERILS OF THE JOURNEY
The design on this Greek drinking cup shows a merchant vessel being pursued by a pirate ship. Merchants returning from distant lands with rich cargoes made easy prey.

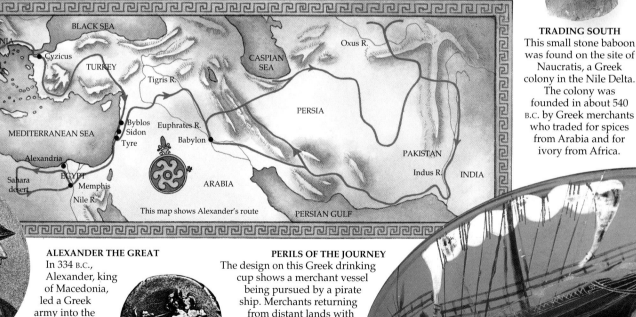

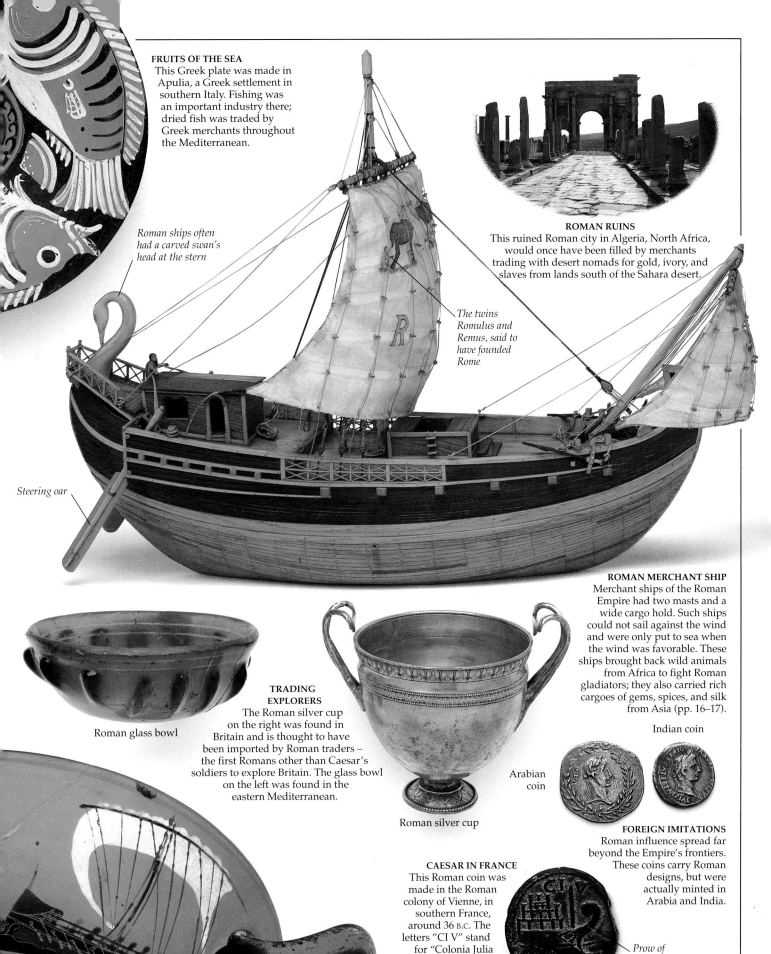

FRUITS OF THE SEA
This Greek plate was made in Apulia, a Greek settlement in southern Italy. Fishing was an important industry there; dried fish was traded by Greek merchants throughout the Mediterranean.

ROMAN RUINS
This ruined Roman city in Algeria, North Africa, would once have been filled by merchants trading with desert nomads for gold, ivory, and slaves from lands south of the Sahara desert.

Roman ships often had a carved swan's head at the stern

The twins Romulus and Remus, said to have founded Rome

Steering oar

ROMAN MERCHANT SHIP
Merchant ships of the Roman Empire had two masts and a wide cargo hold. Such ships could not sail against the wind and were only put to sea when the wind was favorable. These ships brought back wild animals from Africa to fight Roman gladiators; they also carried rich cargoes of gems, spices, and silk from Asia (pp. 16–17).

Roman glass bowl

TRADING EXPLORERS
The Roman silver cup on the right was found in Britain and is thought to have been imported by Roman traders – the first Romans other than Caesar's soldiers to explore Britain. The glass bowl on the left was found in the eastern Mediterranean.

Arabian coin

Roman silver cup

Indian coin

FOREIGN IMITATIONS
Roman influence spread far beyond the Empire's frontiers. These coins carry Roman designs, but were actually minted in Arabia and India.

CAESAR IN FRANCE
This Roman coin was made in the Roman colony of Vienne, in southern France, around 36 B.C. The letters "CI V" stand for "Colonia Julia Viennensis" (the "Colony of Julius Caesar at Vienne").

Prow of Roman ship

Viking voyages

ERIC WAS SELDOM FREE from the menace of ruthless Viking raiders during the early Middle Ages. From the 8th to the 12th century, boatloads of Vikings left their Scandinavian homeland on voyages of exploration. The motives for these journeys were varied. Some Vikings were interested only in stealing treasure and capturing slaves – they plundered and pillaged the unfortunate communities they found in Britain and the Mediterranean. But others were prompted to search for new lands across the Atlantic where they could settle, as farming land in Scandinavia was scarce. The Swedish Vikings, who were mainly traders, set their sights on the lands of Eastern Europe and Asia, with hopes of developing new trading markets. After about 1200, the Vikings became more settled and ceased their long voyages of discovery.

ERIC THE RED
Eric was a typical Viking explorer. He left Norway with his father who was escaping trial for murder, and settled in Iceland. After killing a rival settler there, Eric set sail to the west and found a land with fertile coastal plains which he called "Greenland." He persuaded many Vikings to settle there.

FAT SHIP
Vikings used *knorrs* when on trading voyages or migrating to new lands. *Knorrs* were wide-bellied ships, which meant they had room for passengers and cargo. They were also shallow in depth, which enabled Viking sailors to take them upriver, far inland.

Steering oar

LAND AHOY!
Eric the Red's son, Leif Ericson, left Greenland in 1001 to investigate rumors of a land to the southwest. After an exhausting voyage, he sighted a land of mountains and forests. This was probably Newfoundland, North America.

Steering oar

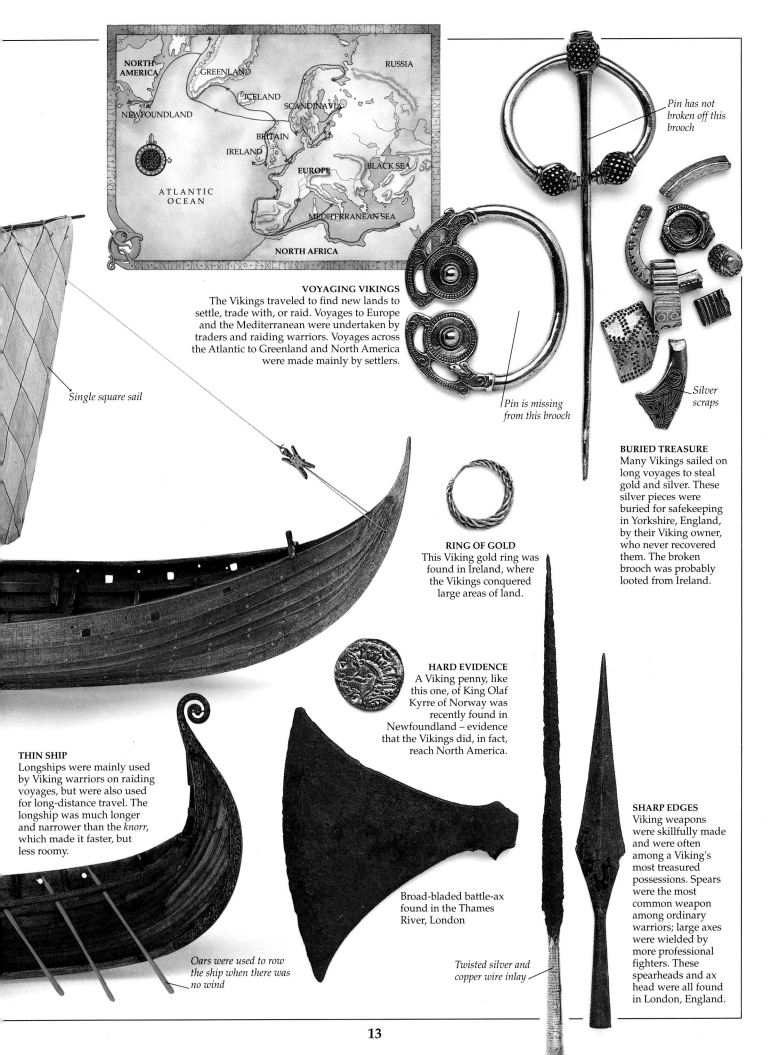

VOYAGING VIKINGS
The Vikings traveled to find new lands to settle, trade with, or raid. Voyages to Europe and the Mediterranean were undertaken by traders and raiding warriors. Voyages across the Atlantic to Greenland and North America were made mainly by settlers.

Single square sail

Pin has not broken off this brooch

Silver scraps

Pin is missing from this brooch

BURIED TREASURE
Many Vikings sailed on long voyages to steal gold and silver. These silver pieces were buried for safekeeping in Yorkshire, England, by their Viking owner, who never recovered them. The broken brooch was probably looted from Ireland.

RING OF GOLD
This Viking gold ring was found in Ireland, where the Vikings conquered large areas of land.

HARD EVIDENCE
A Viking penny, like this one, of King Olaf Kyrre of Norway was recently found in Newfoundland – evidence that the Vikings did, in fact, reach North America.

THIN SHIP
Longships were mainly used by Viking warriors on raiding voyages, but were also used for long-distance travel. The longship was much longer and narrower than the *knorr*, which made it faster, but less roomy.

Oars were used to row the ship when there was no wind

Broad-bladed battle-ax found in the Thames River, London

Twisted silver and copper wire inlay

SHARP EDGES
Viking weapons were skillfully made and were often among a Viking's most treasured possessions. Spears were the most common weapon among ordinary warriors; large axes were wielded by more professional fighters. These spearheads and ax head were all found in London, England.

13

Polynesian settlers

Large double canoe used by migrating families

WHEN EUROPEANS FIRST REACHED the remote islands of the Pacific Ocean (pp. 62–63), they found the islands already inhabited by a people called the Polynesians. At about the same time as the Phoenicians were exploring the Mediterranean (pp. 6–7), the Polynesians were "island-hopping" thousands of miles eastward across the Pacific. These seafaring people traveled in relatively small canoes that were nevertheless strong and stable. They were expert seamen and navigators who could deduce the direction of land from the shape and size of waves and from the behavior of sea creatures. Historians think the main reason for these long voyages of exploration was to find new islands to colonize. The Polynesian population was a large one, and as one island became too crowded, some families would set off in search of the next island.

BIRD AND WAVES
The Polynesians lavished great care on their canoes. This elaborately carved wooden prowboard features a bird and waves and would have been fixed to the prow of a large canoe.

Cowrie shell

Waves

POLYNESIAN PADDLE
This finely carved canoe paddle comes from New Zealand. You can see paddles like this in use in the picture at the top of this page.

MODERN CANOE *left*
This modern racing canoe from Papua New Guinea (pp. 62–63) incorporates many features of the traditional Polynesian canoe. Though made of fiberglass, this canoe is the same shape and has a similar outrigger attached for stability.

SHORT-HAUL CANOE *below*
This model shows a small canoe such as those used by the Polynesians for fishing and for short voyages between neighboring islands. The main hull is made from a hollowed-out log, and the small outrigger adds stability by making the base of the canoe bigger.

Outrigger

LUCKY FISHING
The Polynesians believed that every occupation or place had its own god or spirit. This canoe god from the Cook Islands brought good luck to fishermen.

RELAXING BY THE SEA
European explorers found that the Polynesians enjoyed their warm and relaxing climate to the fullest!

Human hair

Coconut fiber

Shell

SHELL NECKLACE
This necklace, made from shell, coconut fiber, and human hair, is also from the Cook Islands. Showy ornaments such as this were worn only by chiefs and their families.

Barbed point of spear was horribly effective

Polynesian spear

WEAPONS OF WAR
Polynesians lived in a violent society. Warfare and feuding were common; sometimes quarrels continued from one generation to the next and claimed the lives of hundreds of people before they were forgotten. The weapons used by Polynesian warriors were simple, but brutally effective. Tribal armies fought with great discipline and courage, sometimes preferring annihilation (destruction) to the shame of surrender.

Polynesian war club

Shark's tooth

Hair

SWAYING SKIRT *above*
This Polynesian "grass" skirt is actually made from the inner bark of the hibiscus plant (pp. 50–51). Lightweight clothing like this was comfortable in the warm climate and allowed easy movement.

Fiji islander in dance costume

HAIRY COMB
Polynesians decorated their combs with braided human hair.

Polynesian dagger

15

The Silk Road

A camel train

NOT ALL EXPLORATION took place over rolling seas. The Silk Road, one of the oldest and most important land routes, was forged around 500 B.C., and was used until sea routes to China were opened up in about 1650. Along this road trade was conducted between China and Europe. Chinese merchants sent silk and spices westward to Europe over the fearsome mountains and deserts of Asia, while gold, silver, and horses were imported to China. However, nobody traveled the entire length of the Silk Road until Marco Polo in the 13th century. The road was about 4,300 miles (7,000 km) long and very dangerous, and nobody knew for certain what was at the other end. It passed through numerous kingdoms where each ruler demanded money or gifts from travelers. In addition, bandits would often pillage a traveling camel train. Because of these dangers, silk was passed from one merchant to another, with no trader traveling for more than a few hundred miles at a time! The Silk Road declined in importance after European ships began a regular trade with China around the southern tip of Africa.

PURCHASING POWER
Chinese silk and porcelain were very popular in Europe. These Spanish silver coins were sent to China in exchange for Chinese goods. On many of them you can see marks where Chinese merchants cut into them to make sure that they were solid silver!

Check marks

Turkish silver mount on rim

Dragon handles

SUMPTUOUS SILK
The most important product traded along the Silk Road was, of course, silk – like this shown here. For centuries the Chinese kept the secret of how silk was made from other nations.

14th-century Yuan dynasty jar

16th-century Chinese plate made for trade with Portugal

Portuguese ship motif

ORIENTAL PORCELAIN
Porcelain is a very hard translucent (lets light through) pottery invented by the Chinese. It was too fragile to transport in bulk along the Silk Road, but some small pieces were traded since it was much in demand. It was not until the sea routes opened up in the 17th century that trade in porcelain began in earnest.

14th- to 15th-century Ming dynasty bowl found in Kenya

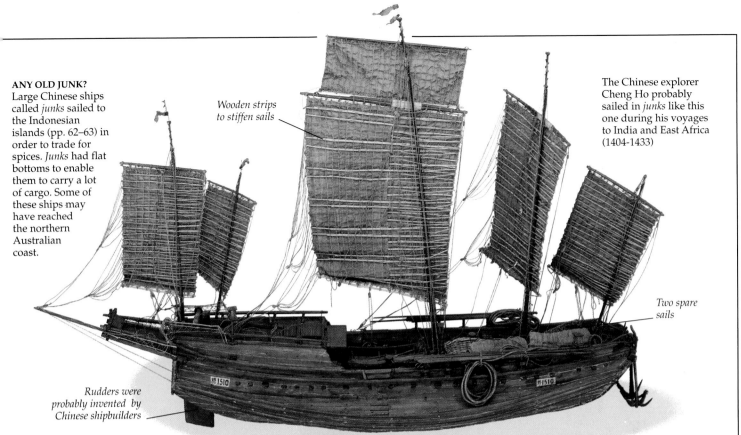

ANY OLD JUNK?
Large Chinese ships called *junks* sailed to the Indonesian islands (pp. 62–63) in order to trade for spices. *Junks* had flat bottoms to enable them to carry a lot of cargo. Some of these ships may have reached the northern Australian coast.

Wooden strips to stiffen sails

The Chinese explorer Cheng Ho probably sailed in *junks* like this one during his voyages to India and East Africa (1404-1433)

Two spare sails

Rudders were probably invented by Chinese shipbuilders

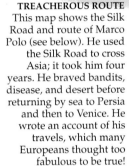

THE RUSSIAN OFFICER
Nicolay Przhevalsky was a Russian army officer who grew bored with soldiering and became an explorer instead. In 1867, he led a military expedition to explore vast areas of Central Asia. He later led four expeditions into unknown regions of Central Asia where he discovered kingdoms and countries previously unknown to Europeans.

This detail from a 17th-century Dutch map shows merchants in the East

TREACHEROUS ROUTE
This map shows the Silk Road and route of Marco Polo (see below). He used the Silk Road to cross Asia; it took him four years. He braved bandits, disease, and desert before returning by sea to Persia and then to Venice. He wrote an account of his travels, which many Europeans thought too fabulous to be true!

The Silk Road
Marco Polo's route

Venice
EUROPE RUSSIA
Constantinople (Istanbul)
TURKEY
Tabriz
Maragheh
Acre Sultaniyeh
Herat Balkh
HINDU KUSH
Kerman
Hormuz
Delhi
HIMALAYAS
Kashgar
Shachow
ASIA
Shang-tu
Ning-hsia
Ta-tu
Feng-yuan
CHINA
Chengtu
Tagaung
INDIA
INDIAN OCEAN **BAY OF BENGAL** **SPICE ISLANDS**

MARCO POLO
In 1271, a Venetian merchant named Marco Polo traveled to China along the Silk Road with his father and uncle who had already visited the Chinese emperor Kublai Khan. Marco spent several years in China working as a government official before returning to Venice. This picture shows the Polos arriving at the Moslem city of Hormuz in the Persian Gulf.

THE ARTISTIC EXPLORER
Wherever Swedish explorer Sven Hedin traveled, he sketched and painted what he saw. Between 1890 and 1934, Hedin made several journeys into Central Asia, exploring and mapping new regions. He was twice held prisoner by bandits, and once nearly died of thirst.

OOST INDIEN.

Arab adventurers

ARAB WARRIORS TRAVELED vast distances to conquer an empire that stretched from northern Spain across North Africa to India in the 6th and 7th centuries. These holy wars were launched to spread the Islamic faith, and many Moslem communities were established. Arab merchants also pushed out in all directions to find new trading areas. At first, Arabs avoided the ocean, calling it "the Sea of Darkness." Instead, they traveled across the Sahara on camel and penetrated central Asia on horseback. But by the 13th century, Arabs were using *dhows* to sail across the Indian Ocean to purchase silks, spices, and jewels from India, Indonesia, and China. Other ships sailed down the East African coast to collect slaves (pp. 46–47), ivory, and gold.

An Arab street trader

SLAVE TRADE
Much of the Arab wealth came from slave trading. Some prisoners were captured in Europe and Asia, but most came from Africa. They were captured in battles or bought from local tribesmen, and then taken back to North Africa where they were sold to noblemen or craftsmen.

MARCHING CHAINS
The Arab slave trade continued up until the late 19th century when European powers took over most of Africa (pp. 46–47). The slaves captured inland were locked in chains during the long marches to the coast.

ARABIC QUADRANT
The quadrant, a quarter circle with a plumb line attached, was one of the earliest navigational instruments invented by Arabs.

Approximate latitude was calculated by lining up one straight side with a heavenly body and reading the position of the plumb line

Quadrant was made of wood or brass

EVER-LASTING *DHOWS*
Dhows have been used for centuries by Moslem traders in the Persian Gulf and Indian Ocean and are still in use today. They have triangular lateen sails rigged on one or two masts and are able to sail very close to the wind. They can also be handled by a small crew. Most of the early Arab voyages of exploration or trade were made in *dhows*.

David Livingstone (pp. 46–47) brought these Arab slave chains back from one of his African journeys

Ibn Batuta is attacked by pirates

BEWARE PIRATES!
Ibn Batuta was a great Arab explorer who spent 30 years exploring new lands. He crossed the Sahara to the Niger River, trekked over the Hindu Kush Mountains to India, sailed to Sumatra and southern China, and traveled on horseback to Mongolia.

ARABIAN NIGHTS
Sinbad the Sailor was a favorite hero in Arabian adventure stories, many of which were based on true voyages. The Old Man of the Sea was a wicked magician who attempted to enslave sailors, but he was, of course, defeated by Sinbad.

TIMBUKTU
Located just south of the Sahara Desert, Timbuktu was an important town. Merchants visited the city to trade salt and trinkets for gold, ivory, and slaves. Some travelers used Timbuktu as a base from which to explore inland Africa.

The Age of Exploration

PRINCE HENRY
Henry the Navigator sailed on only two voyages himself. However, up until 1460 he financed many voyages of exploration and founded a Portuguese school of navigation.

I̶T WAS IN EARLY 15TH-CENTURY PORTUGAL that the first great voyages of the "Age of Exploration" began. In 1415, Prince Henry of Portugal – known as Henry the Navigator – was given command of the port of Ceuta (N. Morocco) and its ships. He used these ships to explore the west coast of Africa, and he paid for numerous expeditions that eventually reached Sierra Leone on Africa's northwest coast. Later kings of Portugal financed expeditions that rounded the Cape of Good Hope on the southern tip of Africa, thus opening up trade routes to India, China, and the Indonesian and Philippine islands – "the Spice Islands." Portugal became immensely rich and powerful through its control of trade in this area.

Crow's nest

Bowsprit

Large hold for carrying cargo

PASSAGE TO INDIA
Vasco da Gama's route took him via the Cape of Good Hope. He then sailed north along the then-unknown east coast of Africa until he reached Malindi (in present-day Kenya). There an Arab navigator came aboard and showed da Gama how to use the monsoon winds to cross the Indian Ocean – and reach India.

This statue of the angel San Raphael accompanied Vasco da Gama on his trip to India

VASCO DA GAMA
Famous as the first European to sail to India, Vasco da Gama made his historic voyage around the Cape of Good Hope in 1497, and arrived in India in 1498. Two years later, a trading station established in India by the Portuguese was destroyed by local Moslems. Da Gama led a fleet of warships to exact revenge, and in 1502 his fleet destroyed the town of Calicut. In 1524, da Gama was appointed Portuguese viceroy of India, but he died almost as soon as he arrived there.

AFRICAN IVORY

Once sea routes from Portugal to Africa had been opened up, Portuguese traders flocked to West Africa to collect ivory. This ivory statue was made by a West African craftsman in the 17th century and shows a Portuguese sailor in a crow's nest.

THE FAVORITE SHIP

Most early Portuguese explorers made their voyages in small wooden sailing ships called *caravels*. These sturdy ships were able to withstand storms and had large holds for carrying cargo. Their lateen (triangular) sails enabled them to take advantage of a wind blowing from the side of the ship.

TIN COIN

By the end of the 16th century, Portugal's considerable trading interests led to the formation of a large Portuguese empire in the East. This Portuguese coin was minted in Malaya (now Malaysia) in 1511.

PORTUGUESE ENTERPRISE

In 1469, the Portuguese king granted Fernao Gomes trading rights with West Africa – on condition that he explore 350 miles (500 km) of coast each year. This map shows the coastline he had discovered by 1475.

AZIMUTH COMPASS

This beautifully decorated Portuguese marine compass was made in 1780, but it incorporates the design of much earlier compasses.

MARK OF THE CROSS

In 1487, Bartolomeu Dias became the first European to make a confirmed passage around the Cape of Good Hope. Before leaving, he erected a cross on the Cape to mark his discovery.

The New World

Even the most educated Europeans knew little about the world outside Europe in 1480. South of the Sahara desert in North Africa stretched vast, impenetrable jungles. Asia was rarely visited, and the stories that travelers brought back were so amazing that not many people believed them (pp. 16–17). To the west lay the vast Atlantic Ocean, but nobody knew how wide the Atlantic was, nor what lay on the other side. Then, in 1480, the Italian navigator Christopher Columbus announced he had calculated that the East Indies lay only 2,795 miles (4,500 km) to the west. Few believed him, and indeed he was later proved wrong. Nevertheless, the Spanish king and queen paid for his expedition, and Columbus discovered America where he thought the East Indies should be. This voyage was one of the most important that took place during the Age of Exploration (pp. 20–21).

THE FIRST SEA ATLAS
In 1582, the Dutchman Lucas Wagenaer published a book containing detailed information about the coasts of western Europe. The frontispiece (above) was beautifully decorated with ships and nautical instruments.

SIR WALTER RALEIGH
During the late 16th century, Sir Walter Raleigh tried unsuccessfully to establish English colonies in "the New World" that Columbus had found. However, he is usually remembered more for the potatoes and tobacco plants that his captains returned with!

HANGING BEDS
When Columbus and his men reached the West Indies, they found the natives sleeping in hanging beds called "hamacas." The sailors copied this idea to make dry, rat-free beds above the dirty, wet decks. We now call these beds "hammocks."

SWEET FRUITS
The New World discovered by Columbus was inhabited by peoples who grew crops very different from those in Europe. These included pineapples and sweet potatoes, which were taken back to Europe.

REWARDS OF SUCCESS
When Christopher Columbus returned from his first voyage, he brought back strange people and objects from the New World to present to Ferdinand and Isabella. The king and queen were so impressed that they made Columbus an admiral and a nobleman.

Royal flag of Spain

THE MAP MAN

In 1508, the Italian navigator Amerigo Vespucci was made Chief Royal Pilot of Spain. All Spanish sea captains had to report to him with details of their latest voyages, which Vespucci added to his maps. Amerigo was first to realize that America was a new continent – not part of China; the continent was named after him.

SETTING A COURSE

Columbus used an astrolabe similar to this to measure his latitude on his voyage of discovery. Because his crew was frightened of sailing off the edge of the world, Columbus lied to them about how far they had sailed each day!

THE *SANTA MARIA*

The flagship of Columbus's voyage was the *Santa María*, a caravel from northern Spain. Like the other two ships of the expedition, the *Niña* and the *Pinta*, it was short and stocky with three masts. Columbus traveled on the *Santa María*, but when it was wrecked off the West Indies, he transferred to the *Niña* for the voyage home.

NEW WORLD MAP

Columbus made four voyages to the New World. Most of his time was spent exploring the West Indies, but on his third voyage, he reached the mainland near Panama, Central America.

NEW WORLD GOLD

In return for financing the expedition, Columbus promised to return with gold for King Ferdinand and Queen Isabella. The gold he found was used to make coins like this one, on which you can see the Spanish king and queen.

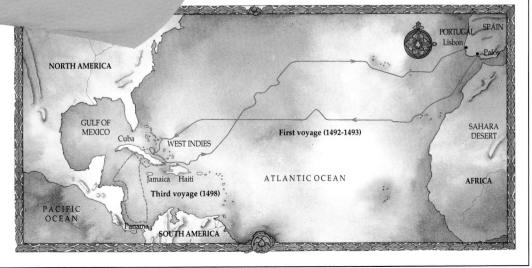

SPAIN
PORTUGAL
Lisbon
Palos

NORTH AMERICA

GULF OF MEXICO
Cuba
WEST INDIES
First voyage (1492-1493)

SAHARA DESERT

Jamaica Haiti
ATLANTIC OCEAN
AFRICA

Third voyage (1498)

PACIFIC OCEAN
Panama
SOUTH AMERICA

Around the world

Although FERDINAND MAGELLAN is credited with having made the first voyage around the world, he did not actually complete the journey himself. Of the five ships that made up his fleet, only one, the *Victoria*, returned after a grueling three-year journey, and Magellan was not on board. Ferdinand Magellan was a Portuguese gentleman who, like Christopher Columbus before him (pp. 22–23), thought he could navigate a westward route to the Spice Islands of the East. By 1500, Portugal had established a sea route to the Spice Islands around the Cape of Good Hope (pp. 62–63). Spain was eager to join in the highly profitable trade Portugal enjoyed with these islands, and in 1519, the king commissioned Magellan to forge his westward route. Magellan's journey took him through the dangerous, stormy passage at the tip of South America, now called the Strait of Magellan. Upon emerging into the calm ocean on the other side, Magellan referred to it as "the sea of peace," or Pacific Ocean. He was the first European to sail from the Atlantic Ocean to the Pacific Ocean.

MONSTER AHOY!
Sailors of Magellan's time were terrified of huge serpentine beasts they believed capable of eating men and sinking ships.

Antonio Pigafetta's 16th-century manuscript showing Magellan's journey

FERDINAND MAGELLAN
Ferdinand Magellan was a Portuguese adventurer of noble parentage. In 1518, he persuaded Charles I of Spain that he could reach the Spice Islands in the East by sailing around Cape Horn, and across the Pacific Ocean. He succeeded in reaching the islands, but became involved in a local war on one of them and was killed in battle.

CIRCLING THE EARTH
Battista Agnese's map was drawn after the return of the *Victoria*. Magellan's route through the Strait of Magellan is shown, but the extent of land to the south remains unclear. The approximate size of the Pacific Ocean is indicated, though Australia and most of the Pacific islands are missing.

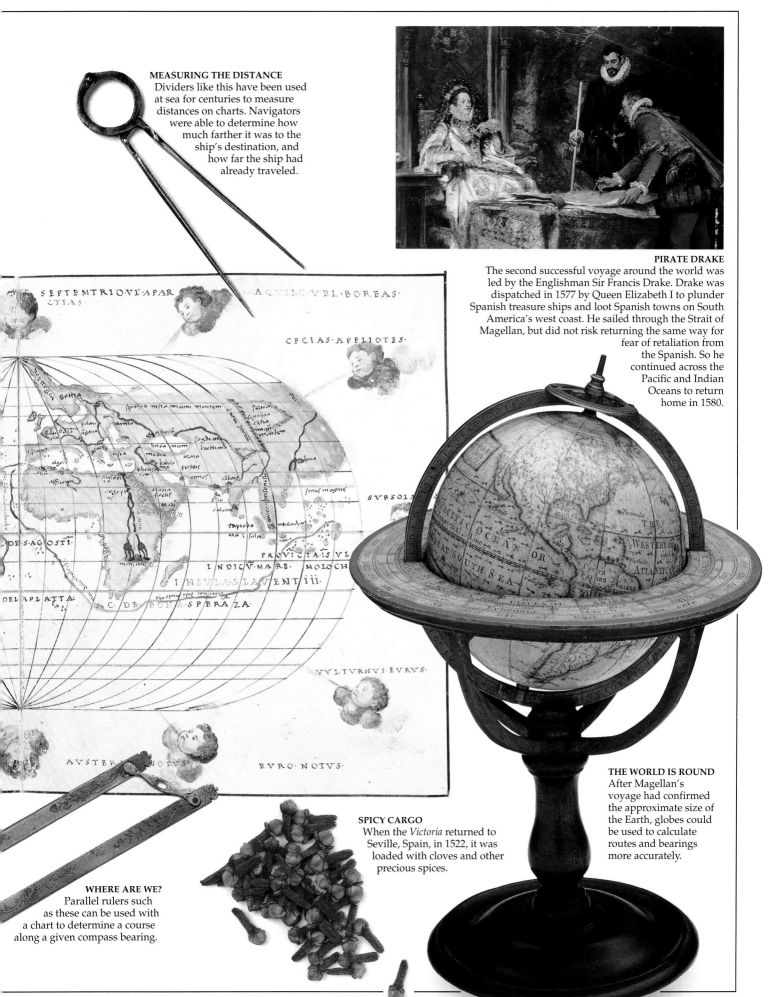

MEASURING THE DISTANCE
Dividers like this have been used at sea for centuries to measure distances on charts. Navigators were able to determine how much farther it was to the ship's destination, and how far the ship had already traveled.

PIRATE DRAKE
The second successful voyage around the world was led by the Englishman Sir Francis Drake. Drake was dispatched in 1577 by Queen Elizabeth I to plunder Spanish treasure ships and loot Spanish towns on South America's west coast. He sailed through the Strait of Magellan, but did not risk returning the same way for fear of retaliation from the Spanish. So he continued across the Pacific and Indian Oceans to return home in 1580.

THE WORLD IS ROUND
After Magellan's voyage had confirmed the approximate size of the Earth, globes could be used to calculate routes and bearings more accurately.

SPICY CARGO
When the *Victoria* returned to Seville, Spain, in 1522, it was loaded with cloves and other precious spices.

WHERE ARE WE?
Parallel rulers such as these can be used with a chart to determine a course along a given compass bearing.

25

Life at sea

Sailors in rigging

BEFORE THE INTRODUCTION of modern luxuries, life on board ship was hard for the ordinary sailor. Long voyages often meant being at sea for months – even years. Fresh food was unavailable, and even drinking water could be scarce. Terrible diseases – particularly scurvy (vitamin deficiency) – were common, resulting in many deaths at sea. The sailor's numerous duties included climbing the high masts and rigging to work the sails (often in the most hazardous weather conditions), taking turns on watch, and swabbing down filthy decks at regular intervals. Seamen spent what time they did have to themselves on hobbies or games, or on playing pranks on fellow crew members. Life on board ship changed little between 1500 and 1850. After this, the introduction of steam power and more sophisticated navigational aids made the sailor's life much more bearable.

PASSING THE TIME
Seamen on whaling ships often passed their spare time engraving designs on whales' teeth. The engraving was sometimes rubbed with black ink or soot to produce a clear image. This art is known as "scrimshaw."

SAILOR'S SEA CHEST
Sailors stored all their belongings in a sea chest, which took up little room on board. These chests had to be strong, as they had a variety of uses; they were sometimes used as seats, tables, and even beds. This chest has the name and date of its owner painted on it and is full of the kind of objects it might have originally held.

GOLD HOOPS
Sailors sometimes wore earrings. This gold pair belonged to a 19th-century American sailor named Richard Ward.

SEA BED
The hammock was adapted from a hanging bed Columbus discovered (pp. 22–23). Because the hammock swings from side to side, its occupant did not fall out in heavy seas.

Sailor's hat

18th-century log slate

Pencil for slate

Twist of tobacco

Penknife

Sailmaker's bag

Fid for splicing ropes

Seam rubber for flattening seams

Palm to protect hand

Needles and case

TOOLS OF THE TRADE
Few skills were more essential than that of the sailmaker. This bag contains the tools necessary for mending sails, repairing ropes, and sewing canvas.

Silver 18th-century whistle

BOSUN'S WHISTLE
The bosun's whistle was used to relay orders at sea. Its high-pitched tone could be heard over the noise of wind and waves better than the human voice. Loudspeakers have now replaced the whistle, but it is still used on ceremonial occasions.

Logbook

Nineteenth-century cat-o'-nine tails

Wooden handle is covered with fabric

THE "CAT"
The most common punishment for sailors was the "cat-o'-nine-tails" (right) – a whip made of nine lengths of knotted cord attached to a handle. The sailor to be punished was lashed to a frame and flogged on his bare back (above). The number of strokes given varied according to the crime, but even a few strokes drew blood and inflicted great pain. A doctor had to be in attendance to stop the flogging if it appeared the victim was in danger of dying.

Pewter cup and beaker

Hardtack

Bone-handled steel fork

Food fit for a sailor

Before the days of canning and refrigeration, storing food on board ship was a great problem. Fresh fruit and vegetables rotted quickly. Meat was salted and stored in barrels. Hardtack was a form of biscuit that kept for years. These biscuits often became infested with beetles or maggots, which had to be removed before the biscuits could be eaten!

BOWING TO NEPTUNE
Sailors crossing the Equator for the first time had to undergo "the Neptune Ceremony." This varied, but usually involved the sailor having to bow to a shipmate dressed as the sea god Neptune. The unfortunate man was then forced to drink an unpleasant liquid before being dunked in a tub of seawater.

WATERPROOF PANTS
Sailors often made clothes from spare materials found on board ship. These trousers are made of canvas left over from sail repairs, and have been treated with oil to make them waterproof.

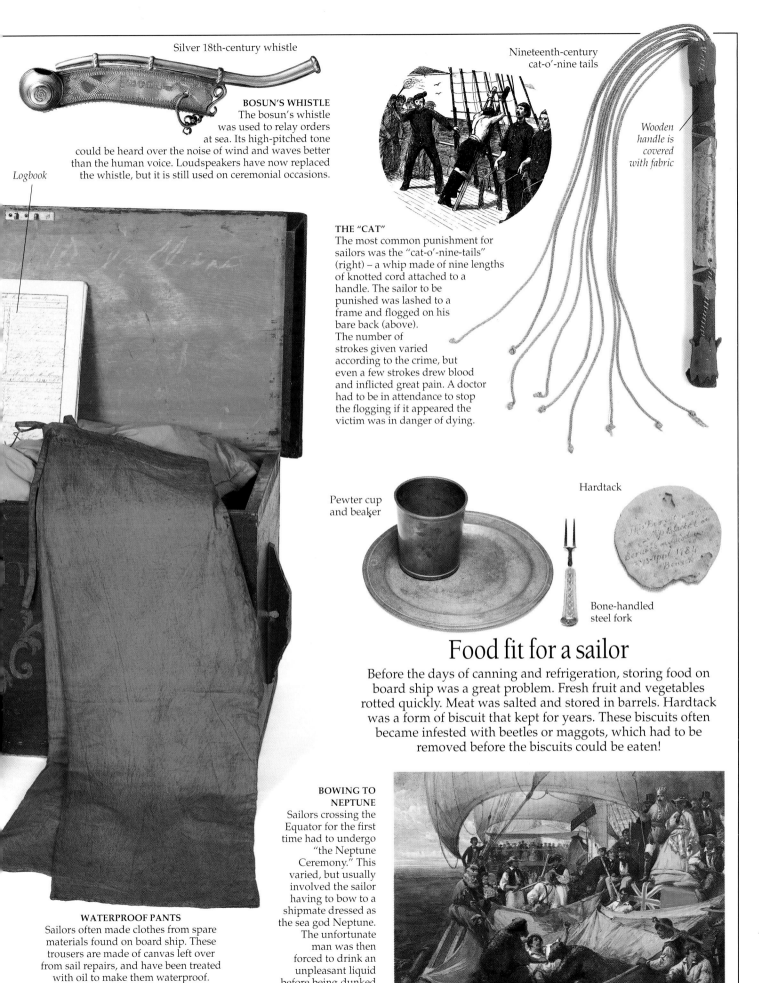

Tricks of the trade

Star

Scale

Crosspiece

Horizon

Cross-staff in use

MODERN NAVIGATORS USE RADIO, radar, and satellites to calculate the position of their ships. Computerized systems can update the information continuously. Before these inventions, navigating was much less accurate. Early sailors rarely left sight of land in case they got lost. Others learned tricks, such as steering a constant course by looking at the sun or the stars and knowing which direction winds blew at different times of the year. Gradually, seamen invented instruments to help them determine their position. These early instruments were very inaccurate – a ship could be many miles off course without anybody realizing. Over the years, new equipment was developed, and by about 1800, reasonably accurate navigation was possible. Even so, much still depended on the skill of the navigator.

Spare crosspiece

Scale

Cross-staff

LODESTONE
Before the invention of the compass, lodestone (naturally magnetic iron oxide) was used to determine direction. When suspended, lodestone always points north. About 2,000 years ago, the Chinese discovered that if they stroked a soft iron rod with lodestone, it too would point north.

Peg

This backsight was positioned at the estimated latitude. This value was added to the reading on the peg to give the true latitude

Vane

Horizon slit

BACK STAFF
The back staff gave a ship's latitude (position north or south of the equator) by sighting on the sun, which was too bright to gaze at long enough to use the cross-staff. The navigator stood with his back to the sun, then lined up the backsight and the vane with the horizon. The peg on the smaller arc was moved until the shadow of the peg fell on the horizon slit. The combined angles of the backsight and peg gave the angle of the sun and hence the latitude of the ship.

TELESCOPE
The telescope was invented simultaneously in Italy, Holland, and England in the early 17th century, and explorers quickly made use of it. By using the telescope, a traveler could identify landmarks or headlands from a great distance and so recognize his precise position. The marine telescope shown above was made in 1661.

IACOB CVNIGHAM 1 6 6 1

CROSS-STAFF

The cross-staff was used from the late 15th century onward to determine a ship's latitude. Navigators knew that the observed angle between the horizon and the North Star changed, depending on the latitude of the ship. By placing one end of the cross-staff against the eye, the navigator could slide the crosspiece until one end lined up with the horizon and the other with the star. A scale on the stick gave the angle.

Astrolabe in use

Mirror

Mirror

Crosspiece

SEXTANT

The sextant was invented in the mid-18th century by the British Navy to replace the back staff and cross-staff. Using an arrangement of mirrors, the sextant can measure latitude to an accuracy of 0.01 of a degree. The navigator moves the index bar until the mirrors appear to line up the sun with the horizon. By reading the angle of the index bar, the angle of the sun (and therefore the ship's latitude) can be calculated.

Index bar

MOORISH ASTROLABE

The astrolabe was an early instrument designed to determine latitude and was first used around 1300 by the Arabs. The astrolabe was suspended by a ring, and the navigator moved the alidade, or central rod, until it lined up with the North Star or the sun. The astrolabe was very inaccurate because it swung about on a moving ship.

Sextant in use

Sextant that Captain Cook used on his third voyage to the Pacific (pp. 34 – 35)

COMPASS

Magnetic compasses were vital to all early seafaring explorers, as they could be used to steady a course. The earliest compasses were magnetized needles that pointed north when suspended on string. Later, the needle was mounted on a pivot. By the 16th century, round cards were fixed to the needle. These allowed navigators to take accurate readings from the compass points.

This log, dated 1770, was beautifully kept with pictures of passing ships and headlands

SHIP'S LOGBOOK

All ship's captains keep a logbook. Each day the captain records how far the ship has traveled and in which direction. The captain will also mention any events that occur, such as other ships sighted, landmarks passed, or sickness among the crew.

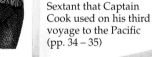

Gold and the gospel

Aztec gold figure

WHEN COLUMBUS SET SAIL across the Atlantic (pp. 22–23), he hoped to discover a new trade route to China and the Spice Islands. Instead he found the West Indies – islands inhabited by tribes with a relatively primitive culture. These Indians had a few gold trinkets, but not much else of value. In the hope of establishing a trading colony on the mainland, Spain sent Hernando Cortés to Veracruz, Mexico, in 1519. Cortés was astonished to be met by richly dressed "ambassadors" who gave him valuable gifts of gold. Not content with these, however, Cortés resolved to travel inland in search of even greater riches. He found these riches when he reached the mighty Aztec Empire, which he and his troops totally destroyed in little more than two years. A similar fate awaited the equally wealthy Inca Empire of Peru, South America, which another Spaniard – Francisco Pizarro – conquered in 1532. Consumed with the greed for gold, many Spaniards arrived in South America. These "conquistadors" (conquerors) explored large areas and established several Spanish colonies.

Aztec warriors earned the right to wear animal costumes by taking many prisoners

UNDER SIEGE
During one of the battles between the Spanish and Aztecs, Cortés' deputy, Pedro de Alvarado, and his men attacked a sacred meeting and were at once besieged by furious Aztec warriors. The Spaniards were rescued by Cortés, but not before they had lost many men.

DRINKING GOLD
In revenge for the brutal treatment they had suffered at the hands of gold-seeking soldiers, some Indians poured molten gold down the throats of captured Spaniards.

HARD HAT
Armor, such as this morion helmet, gave the Spanish soldiers an advantage in hand-to-hand combat. Apart from the obvious protection it gives the head, the upturned peak allows the wearer a good all-around view. Such helmets were usually worn by musketeers, who needed to be able to take careful aim when firing their guns.

BANG, BANG!
This matchlock gun is typical of weapons used by the conquistadors. The lack of carving and decoration shows that it was mass-produced for the army. Such a gun was accurate to about 160 ft (50 m).

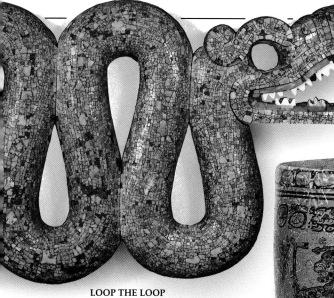

LOOP THE LOOP
The snake was a powerful religious symbol in Mexico, and many snake-shaped ornaments, like this turquoise mosaic one, were made. Many Aztec temples were decorated with carved serpents; the entrance to one was a doorway in the shape of an open snake's mouth. People bitten by snakes were thought to be favored by the gods. The greatest snake god was Quetzalcóatl, the feathered serpent.

Mayan painted vase with lid

Warriors wearing animal costumes

PAINTED VASE
The Mayan civilization flourished in the rain forests of the Yucatan Peninsula, Mexico, where the Mayan Indians built great stone cities and temples; they were clever potters as well. This advanced culture was at its height between A.D. 300 and 900, but it survived until conquered by the Spanish during the 16th and 17th centuries.

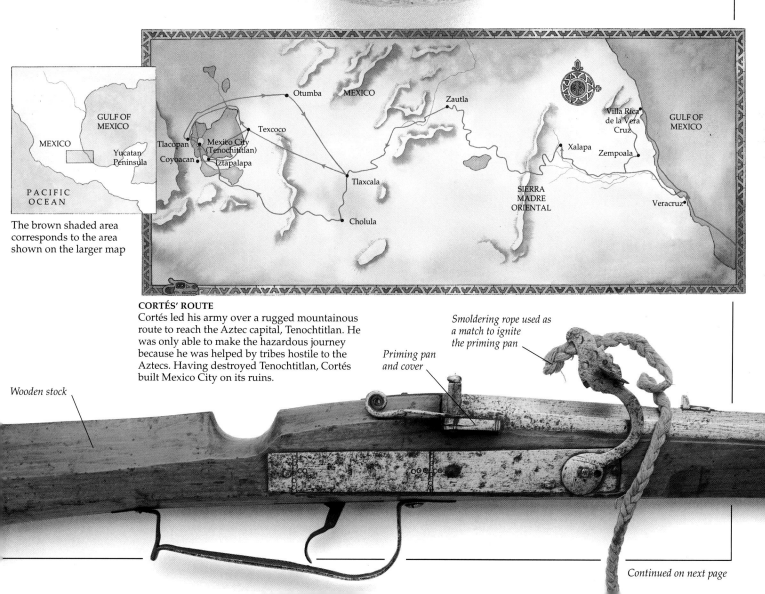

The brown shaded area corresponds to the area shown on the larger map

CORTÉS' ROUTE
Cortés led his army over a rugged mountainous route to reach the Aztec capital, Tenochtitlan. He was only able to make the hazardous journey because he was helped by tribes hostile to the Aztecs. Having destroyed Tenochtitlan, Cortés built Mexico City on its ruins.

Wooden stock

Priming pan and cover

Smoldering rope used as a match to ignite the priming pan

Continued on next page

GOLD DOUBLOONS
Mexico and Peru were enormously rich in gold and silver. Much of the gold mined by the Spanish in South America was made into gold coins which were shipped back to Spain.

18th-century gold doubloons

Lion and castle, symbols of the Spanish crown

Pillars of Hercules, symbol of the Spanish Empire

Pizarro himself is depicted on the large cup

PIZARRO'S CUP
This large wooden cup was made by an Inca craftsman for Pizarro in the mid-16th century. It was sent back to Spain after Pizarro's murder in 1541 by fellow Spanish soldiers in a personal feud. The Inca Empire was governed by Pizarro for eight years, during which time he imposed European administration and industry on the proud Inca Indians.

DEATH OF A KING
When the great Inca king, Atahualpa, first met Pizarro, he mistook him for the Inca god Viracocha, and was very friendly toward him. However, when Atahualpa refused to be converted to the Christian faith, he was seized by the Spaniards and strangled to death.

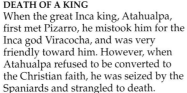

Quinoa shoot

Quinoa grain

"GRAIN OF THE GODS"
The food the Incas ate was plain and simple. Meals often consisted of roasted or boiled maize (corn), potatoes, and this grain called quinoa, also known as "grain of the gods."

TELL OR ELSE!
In 1539, Hernando de Soto landed in Florida and marched north in the never-ending Spanish search for gold. De Soto found no treasure, but was convinced that the local Indians were hiding their gold from him. He subjected them to incredibly cruel tortures in the hope that they would reveal where they had hidden the gold.

CRUEL RELIGION
The Aztec religion seems very cruel to us; several Aztec gods demanded blood sacrifices. Humans sacrificed to the war god Huitzilopochtli had their still-beating hearts cut out with a knife.

THE LAST CONQUISTADOR
In 1540, rumors of a rich city far to the north led to a large expedition led by Francisco Coronado. He marched through much of what is now the United States, discovering the Grand Canyon and almost reaching the Kansas River. However, Coronado found neither gold nor the fabled city.

Catholics use a string of beads called a rosary for counting prayers

The Gospel

The Catholic religion was of vital importance to the Spanish conquistadors. All Spanish expeditions were accompanied by a priest, who was expected both to conduct religious services and to convert to Christianity any "heathens" they encountered. Both priests and soldiers were disgusted by the religions they came across in the New World; human sacrifice was common, as was the worship of idols. The Spanish set about systematically destroying temples and executing local priests, which led to the total disruption of the Aztec and Inca societies. The policy was so widespread and complete that today the principal religion in Central and South America is Catholicism.

The Great South Sea

CAPTAIN JAMES COOK
This portrait of James Cook was painted after his return from his second voyage. His wife thought it was a good likeness, but considered his expression "a little too severe."

Aᴌᴍᴏsᴛ ᴀʟʟ ᴛʜᴇ ᴍʏsᴛᴇʀɪᴇs surrounding the southern and central Pacific, "the Great South Sea," were solved during the late 18th century. Until then, Australia's east coast was unknown, and the two islands of New Zealand were thought to be one. However, in 1768, James Cook, an excellent navigator and cartographer (map drawer), set sail from Plymouth, England (pp. 36–37). One task given him by the Admiralty was to explore and chart the region. During this voyage, he charted the New Zealand coasts and Australia's east coast. His next voyage, in 1772, took him to Antarctica and many Pacific islands, and his third, in 1776, led to the discovery of the Hawaiian islands and exploration of the Alaskan coast.

Dividers

Penholder

Dividers

Parallel ruler

Sector

ABEL TASMAN
During the 17th century, the Dutchman Abel Tasman sailed around the southern coast of Australia – without seeing it – and discovered New Zealand and Fiji.

DRAWING TOOLS
These 18th-century instruments are the type Captain Cook would have used to draw up his extremely fine charts of the Pacific Ocean.

UNKNOWN LAND
This Dutch map of around 1590 shows a land labeled "Terra Australis Nondum Cognita," which means "Unknown Southern Land." Scientists argued over whether this southern land was one large land mass.

SEA TIME
An accurate timepiece was essential for deter-mining a ship's longitude. This chronometer was used by Cook on his second voyage.

JUMPING DOG
Captain Cook and his men came across several animals completely unknown to Europeans. The peculiar kangaroo puzzled them. Cook wrote, "I should have taken it for a wild dog but for its running, in which it jumped like a hare."

DEATH OF COOK
Cook was always careful to maintain good relations with the native peoples he met. At first, the Hawaiians thought he was a god, but when one of Cook's men died, they realized he and his followers were mere mortals. The Hawaiians later stole a boat from Cook's ship, and when Cook went ashore to recover it, a scuffle broke out during which he was killed.

PORTABLE STOVE
Most meals on board ship were cooked in the galley, but the wealthy naturalist Sir Joseph Banks (pp. 50–51), who sailed on Cook's first voyage, prepared his own meals with this miniature stove.

SOLID SOUP
Cook was the first sea captain to take measures against scurvy (vitamin deficiency). When mixed with hot water, this solid soup of marrow stock made a nourishing broth and was thought to help prevent scurvy.

POLYNESIAN VILLAGE
This picture shows Nagaloa, a Fijian village, as it appeared to early travelers.

FEATHER GORGET
The Polynesian kings and chiefs Cook met dressed in elaborate clothes made from the feathers of local birds. Cook brought back this magnificent "gorget," or chest ornament, worn by Tahitian kings.

BREADFRUIT
The large white fruits of the breadfruit tree that grows wild in Polynesia ripen easily and are a good source of food.

CARVED CRUSHER
Polynesian craftsmen were expert woodcarvers and produced many beautiful objects, such as this breadfruit pounder.

FLY WHISK
Polynesian society revolved around kings, queens, and nobles. Only important men and women were allowed to carry fly whisks like this. Strong religious rules called "taboos" forbade ordinary people to use such items.

The Endeavour

The ship Cook chose for his first voyage in 1768 (pp. 34–35) was the *Endeavour*, a rounded, tub-shaped coal-carrier. These coal-carriers were specially built to carry about 600 tons of coal from northern England to London. They had deep, broad waists, no figureheads, and narrow sterns. Cook had sailed in coal-carriers as a young man, so he had experience in handling these strongly built ships. He knew that if he needed to he could beach the *Endeavour* without causing it any damage.

The Crew

As a naval vessel on scientific duty, the *Endeavour* had a mixed crew. In addition to Cook, there were several other officers to help navigate the ship and to make decisions. The sailors were skilled carpenters, sailmakers, musicians, or other craftsmen. The marines were armed soldiers who enforced discipline on the ship and protected the ship from pirates or hostile natives. Scientists and artists also traveled on the *Endeavour*. They did not help with the running of the ship, but spent their time making observations, conducting experiments, and sketching new sights.

Mizzenmast

Mainmast

Spanker

James Cook and Joseph Banks in cabin

British naval flag

Coal

Planks of wood

1. 2. 3. 4. 5. 6. 7. 8. 9. 10. 11. 12. 13.

Foremast

Bowsprit

SOME OF COOK'S CREW
1. Matthew Cox and Archibald Wolfe, seamen; 2. John Thompson, cook; 3. Herman Sporing, naturalist; 4. Sydney Parkinson, artist; 5. Alexander Buchan, artist; 6. Thomas Simmonds, seaman; 7. John Reynolds, servant; 8. William Monkhouse, surgeon; 9. Charles Green, astronomer; 10. Dr. Daniel Solander, botanist; 11. John Ravenhill, sailmaker; 12. Antonio Ponto, seaman; 13. Drummer and marines; 14. Thomas Jordan and James Tunley, servants; 15. James Magra and Richard Littleboy, seamen; 16. John Satterley and George Novell, carpenter and carpenter's mate; 17. Thomas Hardman, boatswain's mate; 18. Thomas Knight, seaman; 19. John Gathrey, boatswain; 20. Richard Pickersgill, master's mate; 21. Alexander Simpson, seaman; 22. John Goodjohn, seaman; 23. Joseph Childs, seaman; 24. Thomas Mathews, servant; 25. John Woodworth, seaman; 26. Richard Hughes, seaman

Barrels of rum and water

Spare sails

Seamens' chests

Hammocks

Across Australia

THE FIRST EUROPEAN to land in Australia was the Dutchman Dirk Hartog, who touched on the west coast in 1616. However, it was not until James Cook's voyage (pp. 34–35), and later those of Matthew Flinders, that Europeans gained a clear idea of the extent of this vast continent. The first settlers arrived in Botany Bay in 1788. For many years, settlers were restricted to the coast, as no route over the Blue Mountains west of Sydney could be found. Then, in 1813, John Blaxland, William Lawson, and William Wentworth tried the novel approach of climbing the mountain ridges instead of following the valleys, and they found a way over the mountains to the lush highlands. After this breakthrough, others attempted to penetrate the dry and lifeless interior beyond the highlands, but some died on their travels. This fate was narrowly escaped by Peter Warburton, a retired police commissioner, who in 1873 became the first man to cross the great deserts around Alice Springs.

"THE SEA!"
In 1862, John Stuart led a team north from Adelaide to find the northern coast. Suddenly, one of the men turned and shouted, "The sea!" Everyone was amazed. They thought their goal lay many miles ahead.

THE ULTIMATE PRICE
In 1860, Robert Burke and W. John Wills set out from Melbourne. Like Stuart, they too were attempting to cross Australia. Supplies and men were left at Cooper's Creek, and Burke, Wills, and two others rode on ahead. They found the sea, but Burke and Wills died on the return journey.

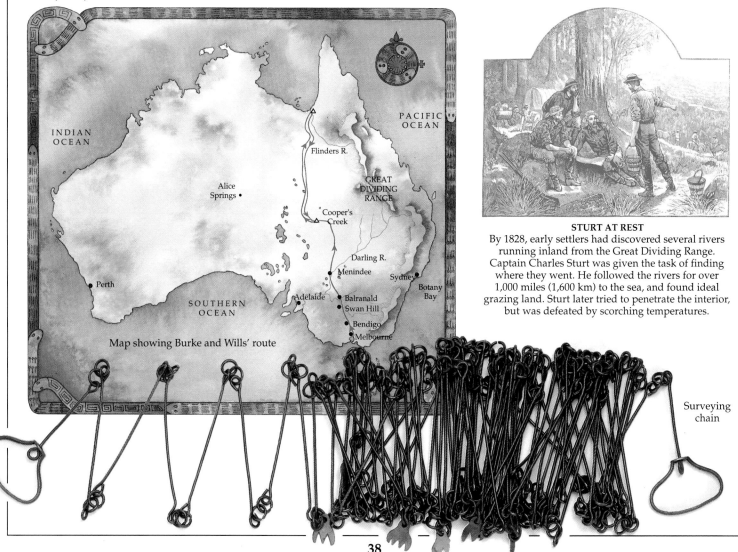

INDIAN OCEAN

PACIFIC OCEAN

Flinders R.

Alice Springs •

GREAT DIVIDING RANGE

Cooper's Creek

Darling R.

Menindee

Sydney

Botany Bay

• Perth

SOUTHERN OCEAN

Adelaide

Balranald
Swan Hill

Bendigo

Melbourne

Map showing Burke and Wills' route

Surveying chain

STURT AT REST
By 1828, early settlers had discovered several rivers running inland from the Great Dividing Range. Captain Charles Sturt was given the task of finding where they went. He followed the rivers for over 1,000 miles (1,600 km) to the sea, and found ideal grazing land. Sturt later tried to penetrate the interior, but was defeated by scorching temperatures.

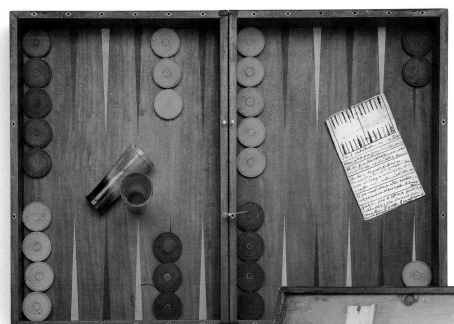

FLINDERS' FLUTE *above*
This flute belonged to
Matthew Flinders
(below). He may have
played it during
his long
sea voyages.

**MATTHEW
FLINDERS**
In 1798,
Matthew
Flinders, an English
naval officer, was sent
to explore Van Diemen's land (now Tasmania) –
which he sailed right around. Three years later,
he sailed around Australia, charting much of
the coastline and proving that it was one
continuous land mass.

PASSING THE TIME
Flinders had this backgammon set with him on
his long voyage around the coast of Australia. It
was the custom for naval captains on long
voyages to invite the ship's officers to social
evenings, when they would play games such as
this. Flinders was also accompanied by his cat,
Trim, until the unfortunate animal was ship-
wrecked and killed off the French coast in 1804.

BOX OF BELONGINGS
Flinders always made sure that his
belongings fit into this wooden sea
chest, which he took with him on
his voyages. Space on board his
ships was very limited, so
he and his crew had to
take as little as
possible with them.

SURVEYING CHAIN
At the time Australia
was being explored,
surveying equipment
was rather primitive.
Land was measured
in"chains"– each of
which was 66 ft
(20 m) long – like this
one (left) that dates
from Flinders' time.
When explorers
found a suitable place
for a harbor or a
settlement, they
surveyed it carefully
for future use.

The Northwest Passage

ONE OF THE GREATEST GOALS of maritime explorers was to find the fabled Northwest Passage, a route from Europe to China around the north of North America (pp. 62–63). The more obvious routes around the south of South America and Africa were blocked during the 16th century by Spanish and Portuguese warships (pp. 20–21, 24–25). Several mariners explored the frigid northern waters, but they were all defeated by the extreme cold and unfavorable winds. The search for the Northwest Passage was abandoned for a while, but in 1817, the British government offered £20,000 ($50,000) to whoever found the Passage. Many expeditions followed, the most tragic of which was that of Sir John Franklin in 1845, from which nobody returned. Eventually, in 1906, Norwegian sailor Roald Amundsen (pp. 54–55) steamed through the Northwest Passage after a three-year journey.

FROZEN SEAS
On Dutch navigator Willem Barents' third attempt to find a northerly route to China (1595–1597), ice pushed his ship out of the sea. His crew survived the winter, but Barents died on the return journey.

JOHN CABOT
In 1497, at the command of Henry VII, Italian-born John Cabot left Bristol in England to find a quick route to the Spice Islands off China's coast. He got as far as Newfoundland (pp. 62–63), which had already been discovered by the Vikings (pp. 12–13).

GIOVANNI DA VERRAZANO
In 1524, this Italian navigator found New York Bay and Narragansett Bay for the French. Here his boat is moored off what is now Newport, Rhode Island.

Handle made from two pieces of bone riveted to outer side of blade

Bone handle bound with leather and gut

SIR MARTIN FROBISHER
In 1576, Queen Elizabeth I of England dispatched Martin Frobisher to find the Northwest Passage to China. He failed to do this, but he did discover Baffin Island, the bay of which is named after him. He returned home with what he thought was rock containing gold, but it turned out to be iron pyrites, now known as "fool's gold."

Map showing Hudson's and Franklin's route

INUIT BONE KNIVES
These Inuit (northern Eskimo) knives, found by one of the search parties sent to look for Franklin, are evidence of the tragic fate of his expedition. Local Inuit made the knives with scraps of steel from Franklin's abandoned ships. They sharpened the steel to produce a cutting edge and attached it to handles made from bone.

Iron head **Bone** **Wooden shaft**

Copper head

Iron head

BOWS AND ARROWS
These weapons were found being used by Inuit hunters ten years after Franklin's death. The arrowheads are made from supplies left by Franklin's expedition.

Inuit in canoe

HENRY HUDSON
Henry Hudson was employed by the Dutch East India Company to search for the Northwest Passage. On his first voyage in 1609, he found the Hudson River. In 1610, he set out again and discovered Hudson Strait and Hudson Bay. In June 1611, his crew mutinied. Hudson and eight others were set adrift in a boat and never heard from again.

SNOW GOGGLES
Arctic sun shining on snow is dazzling and can cause temporary blindness. These leather goggles, which cut down the sun's glare, belonged to Sir John Franklin.

GOURMET FOOD
This tin of roast beef was found in 1958 near the last-known site of the Franklin Expedition and was almost certainly part of their supplies. Tins like this were sealed with lead, which is thought to have caused some health problems. On an earlier trip to the Arctic, Franklin and his men had been reduced to eating "pieces of singed hide mixed with lichen, and the horns and bones of a dead deer fried with some old shoes"!

ROAST BEEF.

LAST MESSAGE
In 1859, the 14-year mystery of Franklin's fate was solved when this message was found by Captain Francis McClintock, who was searching for signs of the expedition at the request of Lady Franklin. The message was written in April 1848 by Lieutenant Gore, one of the expedition members, and recorded the death of Franklin, together with details of the plan to march overland to safety. None of the men on the expedition completed the journey.

One of Franklin's ships, Terror, stuck in ice

ICE-BOUND!
Sailing in frozen northern seas was fraught with danger, and ships frequently became stuck in ice. This was the fate of Franklin's two ships, the *Erebus* and *Terror*.

North America tamed

WHILE CENTRAL AND SOUTH America were
being explored by gold-hungry
Spaniards (pp. 30–33), North America
remained virtually unknown. It was not until
the late 16th and early 17th centuries that
navigators such as Henry Hudson (pp. 40–41),
Jacques Cartier, and Samuel de Champlain charted
the eastern coast. English and French settlers
followed, establishing towns along the East coast and
along the St. Lawrence River. It was from these
colonies that trappers and pioneers pushed inland. In 1803, the
French emperor, Napoleon Bonaparte, sold Louisiana to the United
States for just $15 million. One year later, President Thomas
Jefferson sent Meriwether Lewis and William Clark to explore and
chart this newly acquired region. Other journeys of exploration
followed; gradually the vast interior of the
United States was surveyed and mapped.

**ARROWS
AND GUNS**
While Samuel de Champlain was
exploring around the St. Lawrence
River in 1609, he befriended the local
Huron Indian tribe. De Champlain
joined with them in a battle against
the Iroquois. The Hurons won – their
rivals were totally overcome by de
Champlain's guns.

TRAVELLING LIGHT
Until the 18th century, the only
way into the interior of North
America was by river. Early
explorers traveled in canoes made
of birch bark stretched over a
wooden frame. These canoes were
light and easily controlled.

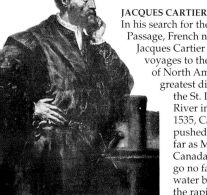

JACQUES CARTIER
In his search for the Northwest
Passage, French navigator
Jacques Cartier led three
voyages to the east coast
of North America. His
greatest discovery was
the St. Lawrence
River in 1534. In
1535, Cartier
pushed up river as
far as Montreal in
Canada, but could
go no farther by
water because of
the rapids.

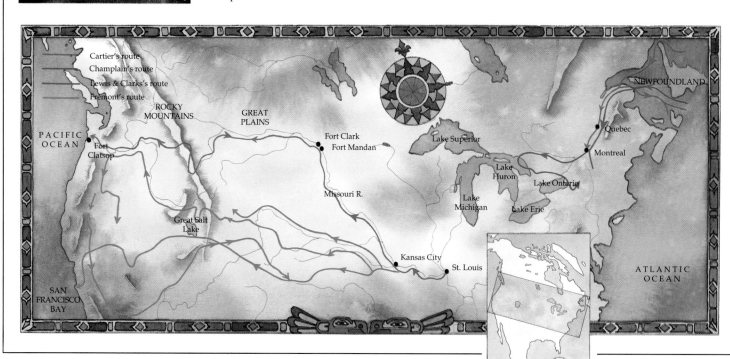

Cartier's route
Champlain's route
Lewis & Clarks's route
Frémont's route

ROCKY
MOUNTAINS
GREAT
PLAINS
PACIFIC
OCEAN
Fort
Clatsop
Fort Clark
Fort Mandan
Lake Superior
NEWFOUNDLAND
Quebec
Montreal
Lake
Huron
Lake Ontario
Missouri R.
Lake
Michigan
Lake Erie
Great Salt
Lake
Kansas City
St. Louis
ATLANTIC
OCEAN
SAN
FRANCISCO
BAY

This token was worth one beaver skin

RIVER ROUTES
French traders in search of furs acquired by local Indian tribes established routes into the interior along the Missouri River. Sometimes they took their pets with them!

Pointed blade with long cutting edge

BOWIE KNIFE
A good, heavy hunting knife was essential to all settlers and frontiersmen. The Bowie knife – named after the pioneer Jim Bowie – was one of the best. The wide blade could inflict deadly wounds and it was tough enough to cope with heavy-duty hunting work such as skinning.

No. 3214 ONE SHILLING Sterlg 1845.
Hudsons Bay Company.
Promise to pay the Bearer on Demand
the Sum of ONE SHILLING for York Factory, in Ruperts Land
in a Bill of Exchange payable Sixty days after Sight at the
Hudsons Bay House, London. 3214
LONDON, the 1st day of May 1845. For the Governor & Company
of Adventurers of England, Trading into Hudsons Bay
No. 3214   A Barclay SECRETARY.
Issued at York Factory, the 4th day of March 1846 by
      GOVERNOR.
      Accountant.

Many beavers fell prey to trappers, as their fur was much in demand

TRADING MONEY
The Hudson's Bay Trading Company issued its own money – notes like this could be exchanged for English silver coins at its headquarters in London. Brass tokens were given to trappers and Indians in exchange for beaver skins. These could then be used to buy food and supplies from the Company.

This scalp belonged to an Indian from the Eastern Woodlands

Birchbark canoes like this were used by the now-extinct Beothuk Indian tribe of Newfoundland

CLAIMING THE MISSISSIPPI
In April 1682, French trader and explorer Robert Cavelier, Sieur de la Salle, stood at the mouth of the mighty Mississippi River and claimed it for France. He also claimed the surrounding land, naming it Louisiana in honor of King Louis XIV.

HAIR-RAISING!
The Indian tribes encountered by North American explorers were often at war with each other. The scalp of an enemy killed in battle was one of their most important war trophies; the successful warrior would remove the skin and hair from the top of the victim's head. Sometimes they would then mount the scalp onto a wooden frame.

Continued on next page

CHARLES WILKES
This wooden mask was presented to Charles Wilkes, a U.S. naval officer and explorer, when he visited and mapped the western coast of North America in about 1841. The mask was carved by Pacific northwest Indians. Wilkes also sailed south and charted the region of Antarctica that now bears his name – Wilkes Land.

RIVER RAPIDS
In 1789, Scottish explorer and trader Sir Alexander Mackenzie set out to explore north-west Canada. He was the first European to reach the Mackenzie River, which he followed to the Arctic Ocean.

Pencil

PIKES PEAK
Zebulon Pike was famous for giving his name to Pikes Peak in Colorado, which he discovered in 1806, and his expedition charted large areas of the western plains and mountains.

MEASURING TAPE
Nineteenth-century surveyors used linen measuring tapes like this one, which was stored in a leather case that also held a notebook and pencil.

PLANTING THE FLAG
John Frémont, a U.S. army officer, led several expeditions into the Far West. In 1842 he surveyed the Oregon Trail up the Platte River to South Pass. The following year, his second expedition took him over the Colorado Rockies, where he planted the flag on what he thought was the highest peak. In 1853, he searched unsuccessfully for a railroad route across the continent to California.

DETAILED DIARY
Lewis and Clark kept careful notes in the journal above of everything they found. They recorded geographical details of mountains and rivers, as well as information about the local Indian tribes and wildlife.

Clark's compass

WILLIAM CLARK
Clark was 33 years old when he co-commanded the first American expedition to explore territories between the Mississippi River and the Pacific Ocean. He was responsible for mapping the terrain and for maintaining discipline.

PAINTED PRIZE
This buffalo robe was collected by Meriwether Lewis and William Clark during their trek across America to the Pacific Ocean via the Missouri and Columbia rivers in 1804–1806. The robe is painted with a scene of Mandan and Minnetaree Indians fighting the Sioux and the Arikara.

MERIWETHER LEWIS
Both Lewis and Clark were soldiers, and although Lewis was younger, he was senior in rank. It was Lewis who organized the expedition and who recruited the men to take part.

WHERE THE BUFFALO ROAM
Early explorers of North America were amazed to see millions of buffalo roaming the plains. The herds were so vast that they sometimes stretched right across the horizon. This painting is by the great 19th-century naturalist John Audubon.

The unknown continent

For MANY CENTURIES, very little was known about the interior (center part) of the African continent. While navigators were charting the oceans, and explorers were traveling across the other continents, the African interior remained a blank on world maps – largely because it was such a dangerous place. Tropical diseases capable of killing a human being within a day were common, and the jungles were full of lions, crocodiles, and African tribesmen who, threatened by the sudden arrival of strangers, could be aggressive and warlike. After about 1850, medicines to cure the most dangerous diseases were discovered, and modern guns could shoot animals and frighten tribal warriors. Africa was now more accessible. While some explorers followed the tropical rivers of central Africa to discover the great lakes – in particular, the Nile's source – others trekked the plains of southern Africa, or explored deep into the jungle as missionaries.

"DR. LIVINGSTONE, I PRESUME?"
So said journalist Henry Stanley when he met David Livingstone in the remote village of Ujiji in 1871 by Lake Tanganyika. Livingstone, a British physician and missionary who crossed Africa trying to abolish the Arab slave trade (pp. 18–19), had vanished in 1866.

JOHN HANNING SPEKE
Speke was an English explorer who made several journeys into central Africa. In 1858, he traveled with Burton to Lake Tanganyika, and then pushed on alone to discover Lake Victoria. In 1862, he went back to prove that the Nile flowed out of Lake Victoria.

AFRICAN WILDLIFE
Speke was also a naturalist. Wherever he went, he made notes and drawings of the wildlife and plants he saw. These sketches are of rhinoceroses.

WHITE RHINOCEROS.

White rhinos are now threatened with extinction

SENSIBLE HEADGEAR
This was the hat Stanley was wearing when he met Dr. Livingstone. Many early travelers in Africa wore these hats to protect themselves from sunstroke.

DRESSING THE PART
Sir Richard Burton was an English army officer who learned to speak Arabic and twenty-eight other languages. Dressed as an Arab, he traveled extensively through southern Asia and East Africa, where no European had been before. He also explored much of tropical Africa and parts of South America.

CONGO ARROWS
These lethal Pygmy arrows were shot into Livingstone's boat on his Zambezi River trip.

HAZARDOUS HIPPO
Like many explorers, Livingstone carried out much of his exploration by boat. He found it quicker and easier to travel by water than by land, but river travel could be dangerous. On one occasion, Livingstone's boat was overturned by a hippopotamus and much equipment was lost.

BATTERED BLUE CAP
Livingstone was wearing this cap when Stanley found him. Livingstone, who once said "the mere animal pleasure of traveling in a wild, unexplored country is very great," continued to explore lands around Lake Tanganyika, where he died of disease in 1873.

Livingstone's compass

Livingstone's magnifying glass

Livingstone's wooden quill pen

MONSTER MAP
By the time Descalier drew this 16th-century map, seamen had sailed around Africa. The map shows the coasts fairly accurately, but the interior is a blank filled in with imaginary features. Descalier had to guess the source of the Nile; its true source was not found until three hundred years later.

BANG, BANG!
This powerful elephant gun belonged to Sir Samuel Baker, who with his wife explored much of Africa looking for the Nile's source. Baker discovered Lake Albert in 1864 and was later made governor of Sudan by the ruler of Egypt.

LA LIGNE

LA ZONA TORRIDA

TROPIQVE

DE:

AVSTRALE

Naturalist explorers

An unusual way of collecting insects!

ALTHOUGH ADVENTURE AND PROFIT were the motives for many journeys of exploration, the thirst for scientific knowledge also became a powerful force in the late 18th and 19th centuries. It was a time when many naturalist explorers penetrated unknown territory with the specific purpose of discovering new species of animals, insects, and plants. Although earlier explorers had reported details of the strange and wonderful wildlife they had found, it was not until the late 18th century that naturalists began explorations with the sole aim of gathering scientific information. As well as greatly enhancing our knowledge of the world, these expeditions often brought great fame to those who were fortunate enough to discover new species.

HENRY BATES
Henry Bates, one of the greatest amateur naturalist explorers, studied natural history for several years before he accompanied Alfred Wallace (below right) to the Amazon rain forest in 1848. Bates spent 11 years searching for insects in areas never before visited by Europeans.

DETAILED STUDY
It was through this microscope that naturalist Charles Darwin studied insects and other small animals. What he saw helped him to form his theories of evolution.

SPECIMEN SHIP
In 1831, the British Royal Navy sent the ship *Beagle* (above) to explore the South Atlantic and South Pacific oceans. It was the custom to take a naturalist on such voyages, and 22-year-old Darwin was given the post. Darwin collected many specimens of insects and animals to study.

CREEPY-CRAWLIES
These are just a few of the beetles that Darwin collected on his journey.

Brass chloroform bottle

Ivory-handled pins

BANKS' BUTTERFLIES
Joseph Banks was a wealthy amateur naturalist. In 1768, he set sail with Captain Cook (pp. 34–35). Cook was under orders to explore the Pacific Ocean, and Banks went to study the animal and plant life. These butterflies were among the large collection of insects he brought back from Australia.

BOTTLE AND PINS
Insect collectors used chloroform to kill specimens quickly and painlessly. The insects were then pinned up for detailed study.

GENTLE PRISON
Naturalists used delicate nets like this to capture insects. These nets are so lightweight that they do not damage the delicate wings and legs in any way.

MARY KINGSLEY
Nineteenth-century Victorian England was a time when most respectable women stayed at home – but not Mary Kingsley! She left the comforts of her home to explore West Africa in search of new animals. Her determination was respected by the men of her time, and her work was highly acclaimed.

FISH FETISH
By Mary Kingsley's time, actual specimens were required to prove that new species really did exist. Mary was particularly interested in fish. She preserved this snoutfish in alcohol and carefully brought it back to Britain from the Ogowe River in Africa.

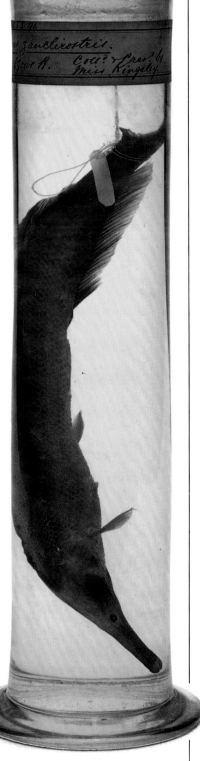

PERFECT PAGES
Henry Bates kept meticulous records of all the insect species he found. The pages of his notebooks, two of which are shown here, are full of beautifully colored illustrations and detailed written descriptions. During his years in South America, he discovered over 8,000 new insect species, 600 of which were butterflies.

ALFRED WALLACE
Alfred Wallace traveled widely to discover new species that he hoped would prove the theories of his friend Charles Darwin. In 1848, he traveled to South America with Henry Bates, where he stayed for four years. In 1854, he left Britain for Indonesia and remained there for the next eight years collecting new insect species and exploring remote inland valleys.

Continued on next page

Plant collectors

The search for new plant species combines several of the most important ambitions of an explorer. By traveling to unknown regions in the hope of discovering new plants, the botanist (a person who studies plants) explorer combines the thrill of adventure with the excitement of scientific discovery. There is also money to be made from finding new plants, and many botanist explorers have become rich through their findings. However, the majority of 18th- and 19th-century botanist explorers were famous only in scientific circles. Today's naturalists campaign actively against the destruction of rain forests and the pollution of other habitats, and they are very much in the public eye.

VON HUMBOLDT AND BONPLAND
Alexander von Humboldt and Aimé Bonpland traveled throughout South America during the early 19th century studying geology and collecting plants. This painting shows them seated among their instruments and specimens in a jungle camp.

Shoot from a *cinchona* plant

Cinchona bark from which quinine is obtained

MAGIC PLANT
Until the mid-19th century, malaria killed many people every year. During his travels with von Humboldt in Peru (above), Bonpland collected samples of the *cinchona* plant. It was subsequently discovered that a substance obtained from the bark of the plant prevented people from catching malaria. The substance is quinine.

PRESSED PLANTS
These pressed eucalyptus leaves were brought back from Australia in the 19th century by Allan Cunningham. He later invented miniature glass houses that kept plants alive on long voyages.

BEARDED BOTANIST
Sir Joseph Hooker was a leading botanist explorer of the mid- to late 19th century. He took part in Sir James Ross' Antarctic expedition of 1839 and visited parts of Asia, where he collected many new specimens.

Sarcococca hookeriana

Hooker's satchel

Hevea brasiliense

HOOKER'S BAG
Throughout his long travels, Sir Joseph Hooker wore this leather satchel into which he put interesting plants he found. Several of the new species he discovered were named after him, such as the *Sarcococca hookeriana* shown here.

Herbarium Musci

50

INTO THE JUNGLE
Naturalist explorers had to penetrate the most inaccessible areas in their quest for new plants.

Pressed eucalyptus leaves

This collection of notes is from Parry's first voyage to the Arctic

Arctic poppy

FLORA ARCTICA
These notes were written by Sir William Parry in the 19th century. Parry took part in five voyages of exploration to the Arctic between 1818 and 1827 (pp. 52–53) during which time he collected and studied vast numbers of plants. Parry's extensive records brought his explorations to the public's attention.

Arctic moss

Pressed hibiscus

TYPE COLLECTION

BANKS' HIBISCUS
Sir Joseph Banks was the first great naturalist explorer. In 1768, he sailed with Captain Cook to the Pacific Ocean (pp. 34–35). He took with him two botanists, an astronomer, an artist, and four servants. Banks brought back this pressed hibiscus from Polynesia, where its inner bark was used to make "grass" skirts (pp.14–15).

Hibiscus tricuspis

RUBBER PLANT
The rubber plant was originally found by Spanish explorers of South America (pp. 30–33). Local tribes dried the sap of the plant to form bouncing balls which were used in games. This particular species, *Hevea brasiliense*, was discovered by the French scientist Charles Marie de La Condamine. During the 19th century, science found many new uses for rubber, and demand for the plants soared.

The North Pole

THE HOSTILE AND DANGEROUS REGIONS of the Arctic (pp. 62–63) were the object of many 19th-century voyages. Explorations were led by naval officers instructed to map the remote regions and to report what they found. The expeditions sailed in bulky ships strong enough to withstand the pressure of ice and packed with enough supplies to last several years. The teams were equipped with a variety of scientific instruments to help them collect rock samples and study wildlife. The men often went ashore on the bleak islands to continue their studies. The long series of expeditions culminated with Robert Peary's success in 1909. Peary was a U.S. Navy officer who had already spent many years in the Arctic. In 1909, he led the first team of men to reach the North Pole.

POLAR PRIZE!
"The Pole at last!," wrote Peary in his diary. "My dream and goal for 20 years." In the late afternoon of April 6, 1909, Robert Peary and his team took the last steps of an agonizing climb to become the first men to reach the North Pole, a huge mass of ice that floats on the Arctic Ocean. The team consisted of his friend, Matthew Henson, and four Inuit (Eskimo) companions, Ooqueah, Ootah, Egingwah, and Seegloo.

ARCTIC TRANSPORT
Polar explorers are faced with the task of transporting supplies and equipment across many miles of snow and ice. Sleds are used for this task. They need to be strong and big enough to carry heavy loads, but light enough to be hauled up slopes and moved by men and dogs.

SEALSKIN CLOTHING
Early Arctic explorers wore European-style wool clothing, which failed to protect them from the Arctic elements. They later learned to wear clothing modeled on local Inuit designs. Sealskin hoods and mittens kept out the coldest winds and saved many an explorer from frostbite.

Tent poles

Sleeping tent for eight men

Tripod for ice saw

Rawhide

Iron-shod runners

Sealskin hood

Sealskin glove

This Boat is left for Captain Parry and his party on their return from attempting to reach the North Pole. It is particularly requested that she may not be removed, as they will probably be much in want of her.

H.M. Ship Hecla, May 15th 1827.

PLEASE DO NOT MOVE!
Before the days of radio communication, explorers were often out of touch for months at a time. In 1827, Sir William Parry and a team of men left their ship, the *Hecla*, to set out over land in an attempt to reach the North Pole. The team left this message on board a small boat which they left behind for future use.

Load protected by canvas cover

SLED HAULING
Loaded sleds were very heavy to pull. The job was shared between teams of husky dogs and the men themselves.

Tea kettle

RUM

Cooking utensils

Alcohol lamp for cooking

Net for carrying extra luggage

Pickax

Shovel for digging snow

The South Pole

WHILE MANY EXPLORERS continued to be attracted to the Arctic regions, others turned their attention southward – to Antarctica (pp. 62–63), a vast island where the climate is even harsher than that of the Arctic. Apart from the lure of being first to reach the South Pole, there was a wealth of wildlife to study in the southern oceans, and the rocks of Antarctica were thought to contain fossils and minerals. Various expeditions tackled the frozen continent; two in particular were led by Captain Robert Scott of the British Navy. In 1901-1904, Scott's first exploration team gathered vast amounts of scientific data from the coast. The second, in 1910–1912, was undertaken to penetrate the interior. Scott led a team of five men to the South Pole, but was beaten by a Norwegian team, led by Roald Amundsen. After the Pole had been reached, exploration became dedicated to mapping and collecting scientific data. This work continues today.

THE RACE IS WON!
Roald Amundsen planted the Norwegian flag at the South Pole on December 14, 1911, a month before Captain Scott got there. He made the journey with four companions and 52 dogs.

CROSS-COUNTRY SKIS
Scott used these skis on his first expedition. They are 8 ft (2.5 m) long, wooden, and very heavy!

Scott's mug from his first Antarctic voyage

Scott's shaving mirror

Scott's matchbox

SNUG AS A BUG
This reindeer-skin sleeping bag belonged to the surgeon on Scott's second expedition. Some of the men slept with the fur inside, others with the fur outside. Whichever way it was used, the reindeer skin was warmer than wool or sheepskin.

Scott's clasp knife

CHEMISTRY SET
Scott's 1910 team carried much scientific equipment, including this chemistry set. The chemicals were used for scientific tests.

Oates   Scott   Evans

Bowers   Wilson

THE RACE IS LOST

The disappointed and exhausted Scott team reached the South Pole on January 17, 1912. On their desperate struggle back to base, Lawrence Oates, who was very weak and was holding up the team, said "I am just going outside and may be some time." He walked out of the tent into the blizzard and was never seen again. Scott wrote in his journal, "We knew poor Oates was walking to his death." None of the team returned alive.

SIGHT-SEEING

This telescope was used by Scott during his expeditions. It was a vital piece of equipment for the men attempting to navigate across vast frozen plains and through mountain passes, as it enabled them to pick out landmarks more easily. It also made the study of wildlife possible from a distance. The lens cover was essential to keep snow and ice from covering the glass and making the telescope useless.

WINDPROOF HOOD

This hood was worn by the Irish explorer, Sir Ernest Shackleton, during his attempt to reach the South Pole in 1907–1908. The extreme cold of the Antarctic winter made such clothing vital. Shackleton later signed the hood as a presentation gift.

FLYING FLAG

Richard Byrd mapped large areas of land and sea and was one of the first explorers to use an aircraft (pp. 56–57). In 1926 he flew across the North Pole, and in 1929 he flew over the South Pole. This flag was flown from his aircraft as he crossed the Poles.

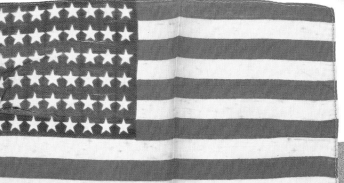

BYRD'S PLANE

Richard Byrd's plane was called *Josephine*. You can see it here being unloaded from a ship in Spitsbergen (pp. 62–63).

Pioneers of the air

HOT-AIR AND HYDROGEN balloons were the only way people could fly until the early 20th century. These balloons could not stay aloft for long, and as there was no way to steer them, they traveled with the wind. When the Wright brothers made the first successful engine-powered flight in 1903, they heralded a new era of travel. Many of the early air pioneers were adventurous travelers who either flew across areas never before visited by humans, or who opened up air routes to previously isolated regions. Early aircraft were constructed from wood and fabric and were highly unreliable; many early explorers of the skies were killed when their aircraft broke apart or crashed. By the 1930s, aircraft were being used to map areas of land. Photographs taken from an aircraft accurately showed the landscapes. Today, many maps are completed with the aid of aerial photography. It has even been possible to map inaccessible mountain areas.

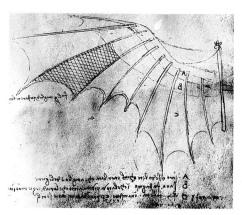

BIRDMAN
This design for an artificial wing – based on a bird's wing – was drawn by Leonardo da Vinci, the great 16th-century Italian artist and scientist. However, his design was doomed to fail as human muscles are not strong enough to power such wings!

LADY OF THE SKIES
In the early 20th century, the world was amazed by the exploits of a young woman named Amy Johnson. In 1930, she flew solo from London to Australia in a record-breaking 19 days. The following year, she flew to Japan over much previously unexplored territory.

Wooden spars to shape and strengthen wing

LIGHT POWER
Early engines were so heavy it was difficult for aircraft to get off the ground. From 1908, new lightweight engines like this one were developed. The overhead valves and light drive shaft and pistons gave it considerable power.

RECORD-BREAKER
Amelia Earhart set many flying records and out-performed many men. She vanished mysteriously over the Pacific Ocean just before the outbreak of World War II.

AMELIA EARHART   LOCKHEED VEGA

AERIAL MAPPING

The ability to fly made it much easier for explorers to produce accurate maps. A photograph such as this taken from the air shows details of terrain that could take many hours to record from the ground. Most modern maps have been carefully checked against aerial surveys.

PATHFINDER

Early aviators used maps like this one from World War I to identify landmarks.

Louis Blériot in his monoplane

BLÉRIOT'S MACHINE

The first sea crossing by aircraft was made in 1909 when the French aviation pioneer Louis Blériot flew across the English Channel from Calais to Dover. Blériot flew a lightweight monoplane (a plane with one set of wings) of his own design. The main frame was constructed of wood, over which fabric was stretched.

Air-speed meter

Altimeter

ALONE ACROSS THE ATLANTIC

Aviator Charles Lindbergh was the first person to fly solo across the Atlantic Ocean. He flew from New York to Paris in 1927 and later completed many other pioneering flights. He also surveyed unknown regions from the air, including inland Greenland.

SIMPLE CONTROLS

Modern aircraft are full of high-tech equipment, but early pilots had to make do with very basic controls. This early 20th-century instrument panel contains only an air-speed meter, an altimeter to show the aircraft's height, and a revolution counter to indicate engine speed.

Revolution counter

Into outer space

THE IDEA OF SPACE travel has fired peoples' imaginations for centuries, but it remained a dream until rockets powerful enough to lift objects into space were invented. Such rockets – developed by both the United States and Russia in the mid-20th century – were based on German missiles developed during World War II. The Space Age began in earnest in 1957 when Russia launched *Sputnik 1*, the first artificial satellite to orbit Earth, closely followed by the United States' space satellite *Explorer 1*. The next major step came in 1961 when a man orbited Earth for the first time. The launching of a space shuttle by the United States in 1981 added a further dimension to space exploration; rockets can be used only once, but space shuttles can be used many times. Current space exploration includes the study of the solar system's giant planets to see if they are capable of supporting human life.

An imaginary view of Mars!

Capsule

Rocket

INTO SPACE
Years of work by the Russian scientist Sergey Korolyov resulted in a rocket that could carry a human into orbit. Yuri Gagarin was launched into space on April 12th, 1961. His historic journey lasted less than two hours, during which time he completed one orbit of the Earth.

Upper section

Hatch

Lower section

THE *VOSTOK* ROCKET
Yuri Gagarin was launched into space in a *Vostock* capsule about 8 ft (2.5 m) in diameter. A huge disposable rocket made up of four cone-shaped booster rockets attached to a central core rocket – and 13 times as big as the capsule – was necessary to launch him and the capsule into orbit.

SPACE SPIDER
On July 20th, 1969, the first man landed on the moon in this lunar module, which contained scientific equipment designed to study the moon's surface. Automatic television cameras sent back live pictures of the moment Neil Armstrong climbed down the ladder and said the words "That's one small step for a man, one giant leap for mankind."

Pressure
helmet

Oxygen supply
connection

SPACE LABORATORY
Skylab, the first orbiting science laboratory,
was launched by the U.S. in 1973. It
contained special sleeping
cubicles and exercise machines,
as well as a vast array of scientific
equipment. Experiments
designed to assess an astronaut's
capability to live and
work in space
were regularly
carried out.

SPACEWALKING
This astronaut is floating freely in
space. His backpack contains small
thruster rockets which enable him
to move around and change
direction. Earlier space-
walkers were attached to
their spacecraft by
lifelines. Future plans
include the construction
of "buildings" in space
by floating astronauts.

SPACE CLOTHES
This spacesuit
was worn by
astronaut
William Anders,
pilot of the first
manned flight around
the moon in 1968. It was
worn as a safety measure
as it could be pressurized
(maintained at normal air
pressure) independently
of the spacecraft.

Carbon
dioxide
outlet

MISSION FOOD
As soon as space flights began to last more than
a few hours, the problem of food and drink had
to be solved. To save weight, many space foods
are freeze-dried or dehydrated (water
removed). Astronauts use the water produced
during the generating of electricity to re-
hydrate their meals. The food below came
from U.S. and Russian space missions.

Chocolate
pudding

Cherry drink

Detachable
pocket

Dried
bread
cubes

Tomato
soup

Macaroni
and cheese

*Instructions as
to how much
water to add*

Exploring the deep

Nearly three-quarters of the Earth's surface is covered by water, but it is only relatively recently that the mysterious world beneath the waves has been properly explored. The first official expedition to investigate this underwater world was in 1872 when the British ship *Challenger* was equipped to gather scientific information from the world's ocean depths. The introduction of "bathyscaphs," vehicles that could dive more than six miles beneath the surface, in the first half of the 20th century was the next major development in underwater exploration. These vehicles enabled scientists to explore deeper under water than had previously been possible. As a result of the ever-increasing sophistication of diving vehicles and equipment, and the subsequent surge in underwater exploration, we now know that the lands beneath the oceans include mountain ranges, valleys, and plains similar to those we are familiar with on dry land.

Mermaids – mythical creatures, half human and half fish, that live beneath the ocean waves – are said to attract men by their beauty and singing

DIVING SHIP
Auguste Piccard and his son Jacques designed this bathyscaph called *Trieste* to work deep under water. In 1960, Jacques took it down to 7 miles (11 km). The hull had to be very strong to withstand the water pressure at such a great depth.

HEAVY AIR
Salvaging items from shipwrecks in shallow water has always been profitable. However, this activity used to be limited by the length of time a diver could hold his breath. In 1819, Augustus Siebe invented a copper diving helmet (left) that allowed divers to work at a depth of 197 ft (60 m) for longer periods of time. A crew on the surface pumped air down a long pipe attached to the helmet. The diver had to be careful not to damage the pipe as this could cut off his air supply.

Helmet is made of copper and weighs approximately 20 lb (9 kg)

Steel ball in which
crew traveled

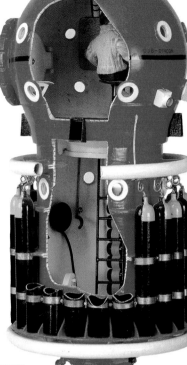

FREEDOM!
In 1943, French naval
officer Jacques-Yves
Cousteau helped to
invent the
"aqualung," a
device that
automatically
supplies air to
divers from
bottles strapped
to their backs.

WRECK SALVAGING
Observation chambers
like this were used
around the 1930s to
survey wrecks. They
were built to withstand
the external water pres-
sure at great depths and
were equipped with an
air regeneration system.

*Diver climbs
in here*

LOCATING OIL
The Seatask
submersible is used in
the search for oil.
Divers can work in
normal air pressure in
the upper chamber.
They have to put on
helmets when they
leave to explore the
sea bed.

UNDERWATER
SPACESUITS
Modern divers
often wear one-man armored suits
like this for scientific exploration
and for work around oil rigs. These
suits are strong enough to
withstand water pressure – and
retain normal air pressure inside –
at depths of up to 600 ft (200 m).

SEA BED DISCOVERIES *below*
Shipwrecks are fascinating to explore,
both for the archeologist and the
naturalist. They
are a source of both
treasures from
the past, like this
pot, and of
marine wildlife.

Exploration routes

THIS GLOBAL MAP shows the routes of some of the most important explorers mentioned in this book. As you can see, early explorers traveled only relatively short distances, but as technology improved, the intrepid men and women who followed in the early travelers' footsteps were able to cover ever-larger areas. Many of them made detailed maps and notes of the areas they explored, and it is because of the information they gathered that we know so much about the world we live in.

18th-century explorers of North America saw polar bears like this one painted by naturalist explorer John Audubon (pp. 44–45)

ARCTIC OCEAN

Northwest Passage

GREENLAND

NEWFOUNDLAND

NORTH AMERICA

ATLANTIC OCEAN

WEST INDIES

PACIFIC OCEAN

POLYNESIA

COOK ISLANDS

SOUTH AMERICA

Strait of Magellan
Cape Horn

Chinese navigators used compasses like this to find their way at sea (pp. 16–17)

Spanish explorers of South America returned home with "souvenirs" like this mosaic mask of the Aztec god Quetzalcóatl (pp. 30–31)

A medicine chest like this was taken on all 18th-century sea voyages

The pineapple (pp. 22–23) was one of the discoveries made by Christopher Columbus in "the New World."

ARCTIC OCEAN

SPITZBERGEN

SCANDINAVIA

GREAT BRITAIN

EUROPE

ASIA

EGYPT

CHINA

PACIFIC OCEAN

AFRICA

PHILIPPINES

SPICE ISLANDS

INDIAN OCEAN

INDONESIA

PAPUA NEW GUINEA

FIJI

AUSTRALIA

Cape of Good Hope

TASMANIA

NEW ZEALAND

SOUTHERN OCEAN

ANTARCTICA

This dog collar belonged to a dog named Mabel who walked into the African interior and back out again on an expedition to look for David Livingstone (pp. 46–47)

Christopher Columbus
Francisco de Orellana
Ferdinand Magellan
Bartholomeu Dias
James Cook
Henry Stanley
Alexander the Great
Robert Peary
Roald Amundsen
Arab routes
John Cabot
Polynesian routes
M. Lewis & W. Clark
Alexander Mackenzie
Marco Polo
Vasco da Gama
Robert Burke & John Wills
David Livingstone
Francis Drake
Abel Tasman
Hernando Cortés

Index

Acknowledgments

Dorling Kindersley would like to thank:
Caroline Roberts, Robert Baldwin, and Peter Ince of the National Maritime Museum, Greenwich; Joe Cribb, Simon James, Rowena Loverance, Carole Mendelson, Ann Pearson, James Puttnam, Jonathan N. Tubb and Sheila Vainker of the British Museum; Anthony Wilson, Eryl Davies, Peter Fitzgerald, and Doug Millard of the Science Museum; Sarah Posey of the Museum of Mankind; Oliver Crimmen, Mike Fitton, and Roy Vickery of the Natural History Museum; the Royal Geographical Society; the Royal Botanical Gardens, Kew; the Peabody Museum of Salem, Mass., U.S.; the Bathseda Baptist Church Museum and the Gallery of Antique Costume

and Textiles. Thomas Keenes, Christian Sévigny, and Liz Sephton for design assistance; Claire Gillard, Bernadette Crowley, and Céline Carez for editorial assistance; Jacquie Gulliver for her initial work on the book and Jane Parker for the index.

Picture credits
t=top, b=bottom, c=center, r=right, l=left
Every effort has been made to trace the copyright holders and we apologize in advance for any unintentional omissions. We would be pleased to insert the appropriate acknowledgment in any subsequent edition of this publication.

Barnaby's Picture Library: 25tr; Bridgeman Art Library: 18tl, 22br, 40tr /Bodleian Library, Oxford 40bl /British Museum 41tc; Hudson Bay Company 41bl/Royal Geographical Society 42tl, 42cl /Victoria & Albert Museum: 45bl, 62tr/ Brierley Hill Glass Museum, Dudley 48cr/Scott Polar Research Institute, Cambridge: 53c; BritishMuseum, London 9c; Mary Evans Picture Library: 6tl, 8tr, 10tl, 17br, 19tc, 19tr, 19cr, 24tr, 26tr, 27tr, 28tr, 29c, 38tl, 38tr, 38cr, 40cr, 42tr, 49c; 50cr, 55br, 56tr, 56br, 58tr, 60tl, 60br; Robert Harding Picture Library: 2br, 11tr, 14bc, 15bl, 18c, 21tc, 21tr, 22cr, 27br, 30cl, 30-1, 35cr, 45c, 45cr, 46cl, 47tr, 47bl, 48bl, 50tr, 51tl, 57tr, 59tr, 62bc; Hulton–Deutsch: 12tl, 17cl, 20tl, 39tr, 56c, 57bl, 58cl; Michael Holford: 6br, 7c; Mansell Collection 14tl, 21bl, 34cr; Museu de Marinha, Lisbon 20br; NMAH/SI/Kim Nielsen 45br; NMNH/SI/Chip Clark 44tl; National Maritime Museum, London: 34br, 34tl, 35bl, 40cl; Peter Newark's Pictures: 43tr, 44br, 44c, 44cl; By kind permission of the

Trustees of the Parham Estate: 34bl; Peabody Museum of Salem, Mass. / Mark Sexton: 26c, 26bl, 26–7c / Harvard University, Photo Hillel Burger 44–5; Planet Earth Pictures/ Flip Schulke: 61c, 61br / Brian Coope: 61bc; Popperfoto: 54tl, 55tc/ Science Photo Library: 59cr; Syndication International: Front jacket bl, 2bl / Library of Congress, Washington DC 10bl/ Nasjonal-galleriet, Oslo 12bl/ 16tl/ Bibliotèque Nationale, Paris 17bl/ British Museum, London 20bl, 23tc, 24cl, 24bc, 30tl, 30bl /National Maritime Museum, London, 34br, 40cl /National Gallery of Art, Washington DC 43bl/ Missouri Historical Society 45tr, 46tr, 46bc, 49bc/ John Hancock Mutual Life Assurance Co. Boston, Mass. 52tl, 63tl.

Additional photography:
Dave King
Colin Keates (pp. 50–53)
Mark Sexton (pp. 26–27)

Maps: Sallie Alane Reason